Collins
Junior
Illustrated
Thesaurus

Collins Junior Illustrated Thesaurus

First published 2005

© HarperCollins*Publishers* Ltd 2005

10 9 8 7 6 5 4 3

ISBN-13 978 0 00 720370 3

ISBN-10 0 00 720370 5

A catalogue record for this book is available from the British Library.

Published by Collins
A division of HarperCollins*Publishers* Ltd
77–85 Fulham Palace Road
Hammersmith
London W6 8JB

Browse the complete Collins Education catalogue at:
www.collinseducation.com

www.collins.co.uk

Compiler	Evelyn Goldsmith
Literacy consultant	Kay Hiatt, Rosemary Boys
Cover designer	Nicola Croft
Design	Sylvia Tate, Perry Tate Design
Editor	Penny Smith
Indexer	Lyn Nesbitt-Smith of Indexing Specialists (UK) Ltd
Project Editors	Shannon Park, Lee Newman, Emma Thomas
Proofreader	Ian Brooke
Illustrators	Beccy Blake, Andrew Midgely, Lisa Smith of Sylvie Poggio Artist Agency, Sarah Warburton of Sylvie Poggio Artist Agency

Acknowledgements
The publishers would like to thank all the teachers, staff and pupils who contributed to this book:

Teacher advisors

Jill Burton	Sarah McKissock
Ruth Grainger	Maggie McLaren
Krys Hill	Amanda Sullivan
Lawrence Keel	

Schools
Hobbayne Primary School
Lena Gardens Primary School
Old Oak Primary School
Standens Barn Primary School
St Gregory's RC Primary School
Vicar's Green Primary School

Printed by Rotolito Lombarda, Italy

Contents

Using this thesaurus

A thesaurus helps you choose exactly the right word to make your writing more interesting. In your writing, do you find you use words like **good**, **bad** and **nice** too often? A thesaurus will help you find other words with the same meaning.

How to find a word

You want to find a different way of saying **hungry**. What letter does it begin with? Use the alphabet line at the side of the page. The green box tells you that the words on this page start with **h**.

Think about the second letter of the word. You are looking for a word beginning with **hu**. Use the guide word at the top of the page. The guide word at the top left tells you the *first word* on that page. The guide word at the top right tells you the *last word* on that page. The guide word for this page is **hot** – it starts with **ho**. Does **hu** come after **ho**?

When you think you have the right page, look at the blue words. These are called headwords. The headwords are in alphabetical order. If you run your finger down the headwords on this page, you will see more than one word beginning with **hu**.

Once you have found the word **hungry**, you can choose the synonym.

guide word

① **headword**

alphabet line

⑤ **synonym**

⑨ **antonym**

② **numbered headword**

③ **part of speech**

⑥ **example sentence**

④ **definition**

⑦ **illustration**

⑧ **phrase**

hot

hot (1) ADJECTIVE
Something or someone that is **hot** has a high temperature.

baking
It was **baking** outdoors so we sat in the shade under a tree.

blazing
The camels trudged across the desert under the **blazing** sun.

boiling
Grandpa hates the cold, so it's always **boiling** in his house.

burning
The nurse laid a cool hand on Christopher's **burning** forehead.

feverish
He felt **feverish** and his throat was sore, so his mum sent for the doctor.

scalding
The water in the bath was **scalding**, so she added cold.

ANTONYM: cold

hot (2) ADJECTIVE
You say food is **hot** if it has a strong spicy taste.

peppery
The meal was a bit too **peppery** for me.

spicy
Dad likes his curries really **spicy**.

ANTONYM: mild

hungry ADJECTIVE
When you are **hungry**, you want to eat.

famished
"Fee, fi, fo, fum!" roared the huge ogre. "I'm **famished**."

peckish
"I expect you're **peckish**," she said, and piled the plate high.

ravenous
We were **ravenous** after our swim.

starving
Starving birds pecked at the seeds we put out in the garden.

hurry VERB
If you **hurry** somewhere, you go there as quickly as you can.

dash
Patch **dashed** off towards home.

fly
Collin heard his dad coming and **flew** to meet him.

get a move on
If we don't **get a move on** we'll be late for the party.

run
She **ran** all the way to school and arrived just before the bell rang.

rush
Adam **rushes** everywhere.

scurry
A mouse **scurried** across the floor and out of the back door.

82

Using this thesaurus

Choosing the right synonym

① The headword is the word that you want to find a synonym for.

② On the same line as the headword, you will see a number in brackets. This tells you that this headword can have different meanings.

③ Next you will see the part of speech. This tells you what type of word the headword is, such as a noun, verb, adjective, adverb or pronoun. If the word you want to find is a verb, make sure the headword you look at is also a verb.

④ Underneath the headword, you will find the definition. The definition tells you what the headword means.

⑤ The synonyms are listed below the definition of each headword. Synonyms have similar meanings to the headword.

⑥ Every synonym in the *Collins Junior Thesaurus* has an example sentence. This shows you how the word might be used in speech or writing.

⑦ Some synonyms have an illustration to help you read the word and understand its meaning.

⑧ Some of the synonyms provided in this thesaurus are phrases, for example **get a move on**. The example sentence will help you see how to use this phrase in your writing.

⑨ An antonym is a word that means the opposite of another. When a headword has an antonym, the antonym is shown at the end of the entry.

Other features of this thesaurus

This arrow → points to a booster. Boosters are lively words and phrases that can be used to replace a headword. Boosters are usually words that are used in speech as slang, in proverbs and in mottos. For example:

---

noisy   ADJECTIVE
Someone or something **noisy** makes loud or unpleasant sounds.

boisterous
*Dad complained the party was getting far too **boisterous**.*

deafening
*Suddenly there was a **deafening** clap of thunder.*

loud
*The boys' game was much too **loud**.*

piercing
*She was a nice girl, but they couldn't stand her **piercing** laugh.*

→ ear-splitting

Picture pages and sections

There are special themed pages and sections throughout this thesaurus to support your writing.

Picture pages and **sections** have labelled illustrations and lists of things such as parts of the body, colours and different types of animal. The picture pages and sections listed on the **Contents** page.

Using the index

Using the index

The index lists all the synonyms and headwords in the thesaurus in alphabetical order. You can use it to look up any word in the thesaurus and find other synonyms.

How to find a synonym

You have written this sentence:

This is a genuine report so all the facts are genuine.

You want to find a different way of saying **genuine**, which is a synonym in the thesaurus.

First, find the word **genuine** in the index. What letter does it begin with? Flick through the index until you reach the section beginning with **Gg**.

Think about the second and third letters of the word. All the synonyms in the index are in alphabetical order. Run your finger down the list. You will find more than one word beginning with **gen**.

Keep looking until you find the word **genuine**.

① synonym

② headword

beginning of a section

④ page number

③ a synonym that appears under several headwords

Looking up the synonym in the thesaurus

① Find the synonym. The synonym is the word or phrase in the first column.

② Find the headword. The headword is in the column next to the synonym.

③ The synonym **genuine** appears under several headwords, for example, **real**, **serious** and **true**. If you are sure which meaning of **genuine** you want to use, choose the right headword. If you are not sure, look up the headwords and check the definitions. In this case, you want to use the headword **true**.

④ Find the page number. The page on which you will find the headword is in the next column.

Choosing the right synonym

● Use the page number to find the page your synonym appears on.

● Find the headword you selected in the index.

● Look for the synonym that suits your writing.

● Use the example sentences to understand how each synonym can be used.

Now you can replace **genuine** in your sentence:

This is an accurate report so all the facts are genuine.

trust

trouble (1) NOUN
Trouble is something that worries or bothers you.
bother
*Ellie had a bit of **bother** at school when she lost her glasses.*
difficulty
*They had some **difficulty** in finding the right place.*
hassle INFORMAL
*"I really don't need this **hassle** today," complained the zoo keeper.*
problem
*The **problem** was finding somewhere to practise his violin.*

trouble (2) VERB
*If you **trouble** somebody, you bother them.*
annoy
*Junk mail **annoys** my parents. They say it is a waste of paper.*
bother
*"Don't **bother** that cat or she'll scratch you." said Auntie Mavis.*

disturb
*It wasn't a good idea to **disturb** the wasps.*
irritate
*It **irritates** Mum if I forget to say "please" and "thank you".*
pester
*Stop **pestering** me. I'm not going to change my mind.*
worry
*Andrew was **worried** by the thought of his tree house blowing down in the storm.*

true ADJECTIVE
A **true** story or statement is based on facts and is not made up.
accurate
*They were able to give an **accurate** description of the burglar.*

correct
*This time, give me the **correct** version of the story.*
factual
*I want a **factual** report. Don't make anything up.*
genuine
*Tales of the explorer's life in the jungle are quite **genuine**.*
real
*The TV programme showed the **real** problems of being a star.*

trust VERB
If you **trust** someone, you believe that they are honest and will not do anything to hurt you.
believe
*You can always **believe** what he says.*
count on
*Can I **count on** you to back me up?*
depend on
*On an adventure like this, you need a friend you can **depend on**.*
rely on
*Now she's ill she has to **rely on** her neighbours to do the shopping.*

a b c d e f g h i j k l m n o p q r s **Tt** u v w x y z

173

headword

synonym

example sentence

page number

Aa

accident (1) NOUN

An **accident** is something nasty that happens by chance.

calamity
*The flooding river caused a **calamity** and the house was wrecked.*

catastrophe
*That plane crash was a **catastrophe**.*

collision
*Mark damaged his bike in a **collision** with the gatepost.*

crash
*There was a bad **crash** on the motorway.*

disaster
*Tom's walk ended with a **disaster** when he fell in the canal.*

mishap
*"Just a **mishap**," said Dad, after his keys fell down the drain.*

accident (2) NOUN

If something happens by **accident**, it was not planned.

chance
*The friends met by **chance** at the disco.*

coincidence
*Ben and Rosie got the same answers by **coincidence**.*

afraid ADJECTIVE

Someone who is **afraid** thinks that something nasty might happen.

anxious
*Mole felt **anxious** in the wild wood.*

nervous
*"You don't need to be **nervous**," said the dentist. "This won't hurt a bit."*

panic-stricken
*They were **panic-stricken** when they heard the ice crack.*

petrified
*Emma was **petrified** during her ride on the big dipper.*

scared
*Goldilocks was **scared** when the three bears found her.*

worried
*Our cat was **worried** when the pet-shop owner picked up her kittens.*

→ numb with fear; scared to death

amphibian NOUN

An **amphibian** is an animal that can live on land and in water.

TYPES OF AMPHIBIANS:

frog

newt

toad

anger NOUN

Anger is the strong feeling you have about something that is unfair.

fury
*My little brother stamped his foot in **fury** when I wouldn't play with him.*

outrage
*There was **outrage** among farmers when the plans were announced.*

rage
*Nobody dared annoy the ogre, because his **rage** was terrible to see.*

angry ADJECTIVE

If you feel **angry**, you are very cross.

annoyed
*Alice was **annoyed** with the Mad Hatter and the March Hare.*

cross
*Steven was **cross** when his sister finished his jigsaw.*

enraged
*Michael was **enraged** when thieves stole his new bike.*

furious
*The old man was **furious** about the broken window.*

infuriated
*Grandpa was **infuriated** because squirrels had dug up his flower bulbs.*

mad
*I made my best friend **mad** by shouting at her.*

wild
*Sarah was really **wild** when her little brother scribbled on her work.*

→ climbing the walls; fuming; going ballistic; livid

ANTONYM: **pleased**

animal NOUN

Animals are living things that are not plants. Humans, mammals, birds, fish, reptiles and insects are all animals.

beast
*Fabulous **beasts** roamed wild in the enchanted forest.*

creature
*Mice are timid **creatures**.*

KINDS OF ANIMALS:

| amphibian | fish | mammal |
| bird | insect | reptile |

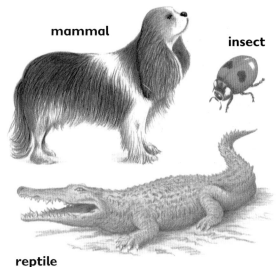

mammal

insect

reptile

annoy VERB

If you do something that **annoys** someone, you make them cross.

bother
*The horse lashed its tail at flies that were **bothering** it.*

hassle INFORMAL
*Stop **hassling** me or we won't go at all.*

irritate
*It **irritates** Thomas when people treat him like a child.*

pester
*The cubs would not stop **pestering** the old lion.*

→ drive someone crazy; get on someone's nerves

appear

b
c
d
e
f
g
h
i
j
k
l
m
n
o
p
q
r
s
t
u
v
w
x
y
z

appear (1) VERB
If something **appears**, it moves into a place where you can see it.

come into view
At last the train **came into view** round the bend.

emerge
A mouse **emerged** from a small hole in the skirting board.

turn up
They waited ages for the bus to **turn up**.

appear (2) VERB
If someone **appears** in a show or play, they take part in it.

act
Our drama teacher is looking for people to **act** in Peter Pan.

perform
I've been asked to **perform** in the school concert tonight.

argument NOUN
An **argument** is a talk between people who do not agree.

disagreement
There was a **disagreement** about the new kitten's name.

fight
We had a bit of a **fight** over whose turn it was to wash up.

quarrel
Sophie was unhappy after the **quarrel** with her friend.

squabble
"I don't want the usual **squabble** about this," said Mum.

arrange (1) VERB
If you **arrange** something like a party, you make plans and organize it.

fix
We'd better **fix** the date soon or there won't be any seats left.

organize
My mum's great at **organizing** things, but she won't do any cooking.

plan
William's sister is **planning** a wedding at the end of the year.

arrange (2) VERB
If you **arrange** things like flowers, you group them in a special way.

group
Harry **grouped** the rocks according to size.

set out
The books were **set out** on the shelves.

sort
Dad **sorted** his files in alphabetical order to make them easy to find.

arrive VERB
When you **arrive** at a place, you reach it at the end of your journey.

come
What time's Jeremy **coming**?

turn up
Chloe could **turn up** any minute now.

ask (1) VERB

You **ask** for something when you want to be given it.

beg
*James **begged** his dad for a mountain bike for his birthday.*

demand
*"Who's been playing with my camera?" **demanded** Dad.*

order
*The highwayman **ordered** them to hand over their jewels.*

plead
*Holly **pleaded** to be allowed to stay up late and read her book.*

request
*The sign read, "Parents are **requested** to control their children."*

ask (2) VERB

If you **ask** someone a question, you are trying to find something out.

enquire
*"May I **enquire**," said the teacher, "why that mouse is in your pocket?"*

find out
*I'll **find out** what time the train goes from the station.*

interrogate
*"You don't have to **interrogate** me," said Nina. "I'll tell you anyway."*

question
*The police said they were **questioning** a number of people.*

ask (3) VERB

If you **ask** someone somewhere, you want them to come.

invite
*I **invited** all my friends to my birthday party at the pool.*

summon
*Christopher was **summoned** to the head teacher's office.*

attractive ADJECTIVE

If someone or something is **attractive**, they are nice to look at.

beautiful
*The car stopped and a **beautiful** woman got out.*

charming
*We had tea in the garden of a **charming** little cottage.*

handsome
*"I'll turn into a **handsome** prince if you kiss me," said the frog.*

lovely
*There was a **lovely** view from the window.*

pretty
*On the way, we passed through several **pretty** villages.*

awful ADJECTIVE

Something **awful** is very unpleasant or bad.

bad
*The weather was so **bad** we had to cancel the picnic.*

dreadful
*Sarah had a **dreadful** cold and found it hard to breathe.*

horrible
*A **horrible** smell came wafting from the witch's cauldron.*

terrible
*Rosetta's writing is so **terrible** nobody can read it.*

unpleasant
*They've painted the walls an **unpleasant** shade of green.*

Bb

a
Bb
c
d
e
f
g
h
i
j
k
l
m
n
o
p
q
r
s
t
u
v
w
x
y
z

bad (1) ADJECTIVE

You say somebody is **bad** if they are naughty or wicked.

criminal
The police arrested four of the men for **criminal** behaviour.

disobedient
I have a very **disobedient** dog. He doesn't come when I call him.

evil
Stories often tell of the fight between good and **evil** forces.

vile
"You're **vile**!" she screamed. "Go away!"

wicked
The **wicked** queen gave Snow White a poisoned apple.

ANTONYM: good

bad (2) ADJECTIVE

If something is **bad**, it is harmful, unpleasant or upsetting.

appalling
Conditions on the road were **appalling**. There were several accidents.

disgusting
A **disgusting** smell came from the cave. An ogre was washing his underpants.

dreadful
The kitchen was in a **dreadful** state when Sanjay had finished making a cake.

harmful
Pollution is **harmful** for the environment.

hazardous
There is thick fog on the motorway and driving conditions are **hazardous**.

horrid
Amy stood in the doorway. "I've just had a **horrid** dream," she said.

nasty
The medicine tasted really **nasty**.

severe
Darren the dragon had a **severe** coughing fit and set light to the furniture.

terrible
The weathermen were forecasting **terrible** floods for the weekend.

unpleasant
Walking to school was really **unpleasant**. Slush was everywhere.

bad (3) ADJECTIVE

You say something is **bad** if it is of poor quality.

careless
Your answers are right, but your presentation is **careless**.

faulty
Robert's handling of the cricket bat was **faulty** so he couldn't hit the ball.

poor
The lighting was so **poor** nobody could see the steps properly.

shoddy
The cupboard was so **shoddy** that it fell apart when I opened it.

wrong
The instructions were **wrong** so we couldn't see how to assemble the kit.

ban VERB

If someone **bans** something, you are not allowed to do it.

forbid
*Our teacher has **forbidden** sweets and crisps in the classroom.*

prohibit
*The council has **prohibited** skateboarding in the shopping centre.*

band (1) NOUN

A **band** is a small number of people, like a group of musicians.

group
*Five of us have formed a pop **group**.*

orchestra
*Our school has its own **orchestra**.*

band (2) NOUN

A **band** can be a strip of material such as iron, cloth or rubber.

hoop
*Metal **hoops** held the barrel together.*

strap
*Strong **straps** keep the luggage safe on the roof rack.*

strip
Strips of gold round the sailor's sleeve showed he was in charge.

bang NOUN

A **bang** is a sudden loud noise.

blast
*They heard a **blast** from the rocket as it launched.*

boom
*A **boom** from the explosive echoed round the quarry.*

explosion
*There was a deafening **explosion** and the ground shook.*

knock
*Suddenly, there was a loud **knock** at the front door.*

bare (1) ADJECTIVE

If something is **bare**, it has nothing in it or on it.

empty
*She looked for food in the cupboard, but it was **empty**.*

unfurnished
*The place was **unfurnished** except for a table and one chair.*

bare (2) ADJECTIVE

If part of your body is **bare**, it is not covered by clothes.

naked
*The baby lay **naked**, kicking her legs.*

nude
*The painting showed a **nude** woman holding a towel.*

undressed
*"You can't come in!" she shrieked. "I'm **undressed**!"*

basic ADJECTIVE

Basic means the simplest things you need, or need to know.

chief
*The **chief** thing to remember when hiking is to shut gates behind you.*

essential
*Water is an **essential** requirement for all living creatures.*

important
*An **important** rule is to check the traffic before you cross a road.*

main
*The **main** thing is not to panic if the fire alarm goes off.*

standard
*Our car is a **standard** model.*

beautiful

a
c
d
e
f
g
h
i
j
k
l
m
n
o
p
q
r
s
t
u
v
w
x
y
z

beautiful (1) ADJECTIVE

You say something is **beautiful** if it gives you great pleasure to look at or listen to.

amazing
*There's an **amazing** view of the countryside from here.*

attractive
*It's an **attractive** village with a very old church in the centre.*

enchanting
*The castle has an **enchanting** garden.*

fine
*It was a **fine** day so we had a picnic on the beach.*

glorious
*"Summer weather here is absolutely **glorious**," exclaimed Gran.*

gorgeous
*Princess Jane wore a **gorgeous** dress sparkling with jewels.*

graceful
*The ballerina performed a **graceful** curtsey for the audience.*

incredible
*It was an **incredible** building with dozens of turrets.*

magnificent
*The king wore **magnificent** robes.*

pretty
*There's a **pretty** cottage round the corner.*

spectacular
*The fireworks were **spectacular**.*

splendid
*The singer had a **splendid** voice.*

stunning
*"Wow! Your new hairstyle is absolutely **stunning**!" said Fiona.*

beautiful (2) ADJECTIVE

You say someone is **beautiful** if they are lovely to look at.

good
*Mum looked really **good** in her new outfit.*

good-looking
*The girl next door's really **good-looking**.*

lovely
*The princess looked **lovely** on her wedding day.*

believe VERB

If you **believe** someone or something, you think what is said is true.

accept
She can't **accept** that she is wrong.

trust
I **trusted** him, but it seems he was not telling the truth.

bend (1) VERB

When something **bends**, it becomes curved or crooked.

buckle
Her bike hit a rock that badly **buckled** the front wheel.

fold
The blacksmith heated a strip of iron and **folded** it in half.

twist
A man **twisted** long balloons into the shape of an animal.

bend (2) NOUN

A **bend** is a curve in something.

corner
The house you are looking for is round the next **corner**.

curve
Round a **curve** in the river was the waterfall where we ate our picnic.

loop
Loops in the mountain road made the drive scary.

bend (3) VERB

When you **bend**, you move your body forwards and downwards.

bow
The farmer **bowed** his back under a heavy sack of oats.

crouch
We **crouched** down out of sight.

lean
Sam **leaned** over and stroked the kitten.

stoop
Stooping down, she touched the track made by the deer.

better (1) ADJECTIVE

Something that is **better** than something else is of a higher standard or quality.

finer
I couldn't have had a **finer** teacher.

greater
After all his study, he had a **greater** understanding of the subject.

better (2) ADJECTIVE

If you are feeling **better** after an illness, you are not feeling so ill.

healthier
Sean certainly looks much **healthier** now.

recovering
Grandma had a nasty fall but she is now **recovering**.

stronger
I felt really weak, but I'm getting **stronger** every day.

big

big (1) ADJECTIVE

Something or somebody **big** is large in size.

bulky
*The parcel was too **bulky** to fit through the letterbox.*

enormous
*Lionel got squashed when an **enormous** dog sat on him.*

giant
*At the end of the party Uncle Simon set off a **giant** firework.*

grand
*The concert was in a very **grand** house.*

great
*There was a **great** gasp from the audience.*

huge
*A **huge** tree blocked their path.*

immense
*This money will be an **immense** help to the new hospital.*

large
*Matt took a **large** bite of chocolate cake and grinned contentedly.*

massive
*A **massive** rock crashed to the ground in front of them.*

mighty
*There was a **mighty** roar from the crowd when we scored the winning goal.*

vast
*A **vast** mountain rose before them, its top lost in mist.*

→ colossal; gigantic; mammoth

big (2) ADJECTIVE

Sometimes **big** can mean important, or having a lot of influence.

important
*"Hey, I think we've found something **important**," said Carter.*

serious
*Burglary is a **serious** problem in this area.*

bin VERB

If you **bin** something, you throw it away.

discard
*Mum tried to persuade Dad to **discard** his old jacket.*

scrap
*She decided to **scrap** everything she'd written so far.*

bind VERB

If you **bind** something, you tie something like string or cloth tightly round it so that it is held in place.

attach
*In our first-aid class, we were taught to **attach** splints to a damaged limb.*

fasten
*The woodcutter always **fastens** the firewood with twine.*

join
*Simon used extra-strong tape to **join** the broken struts together.*

tie
*"I'll **tie** a handkerchief round your leg to stop the bleeding," said Mum.*

bird NOUN

A **bird** is an animal with two legs, two wings and feathers.

PET BIRDS:
budgerigar
cockatiel

budgerigar

FARM BIRDS:
chicken   goose
duck   turkey

duck

BRITISH GARDEN BIRDS:
blackbird
blue tit
chaffinch
robin
sparrow
thrush
wren

robin

BIRDS OF PREY:
buzzard
eagle
falcon
kestrel
owl

kestrel

BIRDS THAT LIVE NEAR WATER:
coot   moorhen
curlew   pelican
duck   penguin
flamingo   puffin
goose   stork
gull   swan
kingfisher

kingfisher

OTHER BIRDS:
emu
kiwi
kookaburra
ostrich
parrot
peacock
vulture

peacock

bit NOUN

A **bit** of something is a small piece of it.

chip
We found a **chip** of Roman pottery in the garden.

chunk
Henry broke off a **chunk** of chocolate.

crumb
Under the table, birds were pecking at leftover **crumbs**.

fragment
They were looking for fossils but found only a small **fragment** of bone.

morsel
Oliver was so hungry he ate up every last **morsel** of pie.

part
Julia liked the **part** in the film where owls brought messages.

piece
She couldn't finish the jigsaw. There was one **piece** missing.

portion
Every guest had a **portion** of cheese.

scrap
There was an interesting **scrap** of paper at the crime scene.

shred
The kitten tore the curtains to **shreds**.

slab
A **slab** of white stone covered the mouth of the tomb.

speck
If there was a **speck** of dust my mum would find it.

body

body NOUN
Your **body** is every part of you.

forehead

head

hair

eyelid

eyebrow

pupil

eye

iris

hand

eyelashes

nose

ear

nostril

cheek

mouth

palm

teeth

lip

chin

wrist

neck

elbow

shoulder

armpit

chest

stomach

waist

arm

navel

hip

finger

thumb

thigh

fingernail

leg

knee

shin

calf

toe

ankle

heel

foot

boil VERB

When liquid **boils**, it bubbles.

bubble
*Stew **bubbled** furiously on the stove.*

foam
*Warm the butter until it **foams**.*

froth
*Hot milk rose in the pan and **frothed** over the top.*

heat
***Heat** the mixture for five minutes.*

book NOUN

A **book** is a number of pages held together inside a cover.

KINDS OF BOOKS:

album	manual
atlas	notebook
diary	novel
dictionary	storybook
encyclopedia	textbook
jotter	thesaurus

boring ADJECTIVE

Something **boring** is so dull that you have no interest in it.

dreary
*We spent a **dreary** afternoon queuing for concert tickets.*

dull
*The film was so **dull** that William fell asleep in the middle of it.*

monotonous
*The television presenter droned on in a **monotonous** voice.*

➜ mind-numbing

ANTONYM: **exciting**

bottom (1) NOUN

The **bottom** of something is the lowest part of it.

base
*There were lots of fallen rocks at the **base** of the cliff.*

bed
*The **bed** of the river was sandy.*

foot
*They stopped at the **foot** of the mountain and looked up.*

foundation
*It was an old pillar. The **foundation** was crumbling.*

bottom (2) NOUN

Your **bottom** is the part of your body that you sit on.

behind
*Llewelyn sat there so long that his **behind** went numb.*

bum INFORMAL
*"Does my **bum** look big in this?" Abdul's teenage sister asked.*

buttocks
*A fall on the ice bruised his **buttocks**.*

rear
*While Tom was looking round the farm, a goat butted him in the **rear**.*

a
Bb
c
d
e
f
g
h
i
j
k
l
m
n
o
p
q
r
s
t
u
v
w
x
y
z

box NOUN

A **box** is a container with straight sides, made from something stiff, like cardboard, wood or plastic.

carton
They took a **carton** of strawberries with them on the picnic.

case
When we moved, all our books were packed in **cases**.

chest
Tommy keeps his toys in a **chest**.

packet
Sarah wanted her own small **packet** of cereal for breakfast.

brave ADJECTIVE

If you are **brave**, you show you can do something even if it is frightening.

adventurous
Alice was **adventurous** and liked to try new things.

bold
The kitten was **bold** enough to tap the dog on its nose.

courageous
The **courageous** dentist agreed to check the lion's teeth.

daring
King Arthur's knights did all sorts of **daring** deeds.

fearless
People doing extreme sports seem **fearless**.

→ heroic; intrepid

ANTONYM: **cowardly**

break (1) VERB

If you **break** something, it splits into pieces or stops working.

chip
"Don't bang that plate down or you'll **chip** it," said Mum.

crack
The ogre gazed at his reflection. This made the mirror **crack**.

crumble
She sat anxiously **crumbling** a piece of bread in her fingers.

fall apart
Jeremy gloomily watched his bookshelves **fall apart**.

shatter
Her voice is so loud it could **shatter** glass.

smash
The guard saw the priceless statue **smash** on the ground.

snap
Simone heard a twig **snap** behind her. She spun round in alarm.

splinter
The Snow Queen made the glass **splinter** into a thousand fragments.

break (2) NOUN

A **break** is a short rest or change.

interval
In the play there's a short **interval** between two acts.

pause
There was a **pause** while the teacher hunted for her notes.

rest
"I'm exhausted," said Daniel. "Let's have a **rest** before we go out."

bright (1) ADJECTIVE

Someone who is **bright** is quick at learning or noticing things.

brainy
*My brother's really **brainy**. He wants to go to university.*

clever
*"If you're **clever**, you'll put the watch together again," said Jessie.*

intelligent
*Guide dogs have to be very **intelligent**.*

sharp
*"You're very **sharp**," said the old lady, "but you still haven't solved the puzzle."*

smart
*Some people think squirrels are **smart**, but they often can't find nuts they've buried.*

bright (2) ADJECTIVE

Bright lights and colours are strong and startling.

brilliant
*Parrots' **brilliant** colours make them easy to see.*

colourful
*The magician produced a **colourful** string of knotted scarves.*

dazzling
*They shaded their eyes against his **dazzling** white shirt.*

glaring
***Glaring** headlights blinded Dad and he had to stop the car.*

glowing
*The bonfire was **glowing** in the dark.*

bright (3) ADJECTIVE

Someone who is **bright** is cheerful and lively.

cheerful
*I like Alex. He's always so **cheerful** and jolly in class.*

lively
*Kamal felt **lively** and refreshed when he woke up.*

bring VERB

If you **bring** something or someone, you have them with you when you arrive.

carry
*He arrived **carrying** presents for everyone.*

guide
*You'll need someone to **guide** you back if it's dark.*

lead
*Firemen often have to **lead** people out of burning buildings.*

take
*Taxis were used to **take** guests to the wedding reception.*

build VERB

If you **build** something, you make it by joining things together.

create
*Dad **created** a wonderful tree house for us.*

make
*The children **made** an igloo with small blocks of snow.*

put up
*We **put up** a fence round the guinea pigs to keep them safe.*

building

a

Bb

c

d

e

f

g

h

i

j

k

l

m

n

o

p

q

r

s

t

u

v

w

x

y

z

building NOUN

A **building** is a place, such as a house, that has walls and a roof.

BUILDINGS TO LIVE IN:

apartment	detached house
bungalow	flat
castle	semi-detached house
cottage	terraced house

castle

terraced houses

cottage

BUILDINGS TO WORK IN:

factory
fire station
garage
hospital
laboratory
library
lighthouse
police station
shop
skyscraper
studio
windmill

windmill

skyscraper

lighthouse

BUILDINGS TO WORSHIP IN:

cathedral
chapel
church
mosque
synagogue
temple

mosque

cathedral

temple

bully VERB
Someone who **bullies** people hurts or frightens them.

frighten
The witch **frightened** him into helping her gather mushrooms.

threaten
One of the big boys **threatened** us.

torment
Stop **tormenting** your little sister.

bump NOUN
A **bump** is a raised, uneven part on a surface.

bulge
A bag of sweets made a **bulge** in his jacket pocket.

hump
There are **humps** here to slow down traffic.

lump
Our old mattress is full of **lumps**.

swelling
Chloe had a nasty **swelling** on her finger.

bump into VERB
If you **bump into** something, you hit it while you are moving.

bang into
The brakes on his bike failed and he **banged into** the fence.

collide with
In the dark our car **collided with** a tree.

hit
He ran into the road without looking and **hit** a cyclist.

strike
She **struck** a litterbin when she lost control of her skateboard.

bunch NOUN
A **bunch** is a group of things together, like flowers or grapes.

bouquet
The bride carried a **bouquet** of roses.

posy
Emma gave her mum a lovely **posy** of bright flowers.

spray
Sprays of holly brightened the hall.

bundle NOUN
A **bundle** is a number of small things gathered together.

batch
The first **batch** of letters arrived next day.

collection
We put a **collection** of newspapers out for recycling.

heap
On the table was a **heap** of clothes for the charity shop.

pile
A **pile** of dirty washing was waiting to go to the launderette.

burn VERB
If something is **burning**, it is on fire.

blaze
A bonfire **blazed** in the garden.

flame
The fire began to **flame** green as it caught the ink.

flare
Suddenly a match **flared** in the darkness.

flicker
He blew gently on the spark and the fire began to **flicker**.

burst VERB
When something like a balloon or tyre **bursts**, it splits apart suddenly.

explode
One of the bottles **exploded** in the heat.

pop
The baby laughed with delight when the bubbles **popped**.

puncture
A nail **punctured** one of my tyres.

a
b
Cc
d
e
f
g
h
i
j
k
l
m
n
o
p
q
r
s
t
u
v
w
x
y
z

Cc

call (1) VERB

If you **call**, you phone or visit someone.

phone
I'll phone you as soon as I get there.

ring
Give me a ring one day next week.

visit
Grandpa wants us to visit tomorrow.

call (2) VERB

If you **call** someone, you shout for them.

cry
"Where are you hiding?" she cried.

cry out
Rashid cried out in delight when he saw the otter.

shout
"Come on Ben. You'll be late for school," Mum shouted.

yell
"Come on in!" Tracy yelled. "The water is great!"

calm (1) ADJECTIVE

If something is **calm**, it is still and peaceful.

peaceful
Everything seemed peaceful in the church.

still
That afternoon the breeze had dropped and the air was still.

calm (2) ADJECTIVE

If you are **calm**, you do not seem worried or excited.

cool
She was surprisingly cool about the exciting news.

quiet
The children were very quiet until they saw the mouse.

car NOUN

A **car** is a road vehicle with wheels and an engine. It needs a driver and usually has room for passengers.

KINDS OF CARS:

convertible	people carrier
estate	racing car
four-wheel drive	saloon
hatchback	sports car
limousine	taxi
minicab	vintage car

vintage car

care VERB

If you **care** about something, you are concerned about it.

be bothered
I am bothered about missing my swimming lessons.

be concerned
My brother is concerned about the world's endangered wildlife.

mind
Gavin said he didn't mind who won the game of chess.

careful (1) ADJECTIVE

If you are **careful**, you try to do things well.

accurate
The soldier had to be accurate. He had only one chance to hit the target.

thorough
We made a thorough search of the room.

careful (2) ADJECTIVE

If you are **careful**, you try to do things safely.

alert
In Australia there is a danger of bush fires, and people have to be alert.

cautious
The lifeguard taught them to be cautious around the pool.

wary
Joe knew he had to be wary of strangers.

watchful
With a toddler, you have to be watchful all the time.

careless (1) ADJECTIVE

If you are **careless**, you do not take enough care.

messy
My little sister is a messy eater.

sloppy
Her knitting was sloppy, with dropped stitches everywhere.

untidy
The professor was untidy. Now he couldn't find his papers.

careless (2) ADJECTIVE

Careless can also mean not being sensible about things.

reckless
Sam took a reckless leap over the river.

thoughtless
Only thoughtless people went out in the storm without a jacket.

carry VERB

When you **carry** something, you pick it up and take it with you.

move
He moved the plant over to the window.

take
We'd better take an umbrella.

transport
We need a van to transport our furniture.

catch (1) VERB

If you catch something, like measles, you get that illness.

come down with
"Stay away from me or you'll come down with chickenpox too," said Beth.

get
I don't want to get his cold.

go down with
It's just like Ross to go down with something at the wrong moment.

catch (2) VERB

If you **catch** somebody or something, you capture them.

arrest
The police want to arrest a man they suspect of burglary.

capture
Prison guards set a trap to capture the escaped prisoner.

trap
"Trap that spider," said Granny, "then put it outside."

a
b
Cc
d
e
f
g
h
i
j
k
l
m
n
o
p
q
r
s
t
u
v
w
x
y
z

change

change (1) VERB

When you **change** something, it becomes different.

alter
*The tailor said he could soon **alter** the length of the trouser legs.*

modify
*Let's **modify** the plan. We'll go this afternoon instead.*

reorganize
*"Oh no!" cried Mrs Jones. "I'm going to have to **reorganize** everything."*

revise
*The teacher said my story was good, but I should **revise** the ending.*

change (2) VERB

When something **changes**, it becomes different.

develop
*Tadpoles soon **develop** into frogs.*

shift
*The wind **shifted** to the west.*

turn
*Caterpillars **turn** into moths or butterflies.*

change (3) VERB

If you **change** something, you replace it with something else.

exchange
*"Can I **exchange** this blue shirt for a green one?" asked the customer.*

swap
*Henry wanted to **swap** his pop music CD for one of Rosie's.*

switch
*I didn't see him **switch** his old pen for my new one.*

chase VERB

If you **chase** someone, you try to catch them.

follow
*The boys **followed** the man they suspected of stealing a bike.*

hunt
*Our cat was out all night, **hunting** mice and rats.*

pursue
*Police **pursued** the speeding car for miles along the motorway.*

trail
*It was easy to **trail** the robber by following his footprints in the snow.*

check VERB

If you **check** something, you make sure it is correct and safe.

examine
*The witch frowned and **examined** the contents of the cauldron.*

inspect
*The mechanic **inspected** the car's brakes.*

make sure
*Before we set off, I **made sure** we'd remembered everything.*

test
*He **tested** the ground in case it was boggy.*

choose VERB

When you **choose**, you decide what to have or do.

elect
*They quickly **elected** a new leader.*

name
*Each one **named** the person they wanted.*

pick
*He **picked** the biggest cake he could find.*

select
*They were told to **select** a book and read for the rest of the lesson.*

take
*We **took** the shortest way.*

clean (1) VERB

If you **clean** something, you remove dirt from it.

DIFFERENT WAYS OF CLEANING:

bathe	scrub
brush	shampoo
dust	sponge
mop up	sweep
polish	vacuum
rinse	wash
scour	wipe

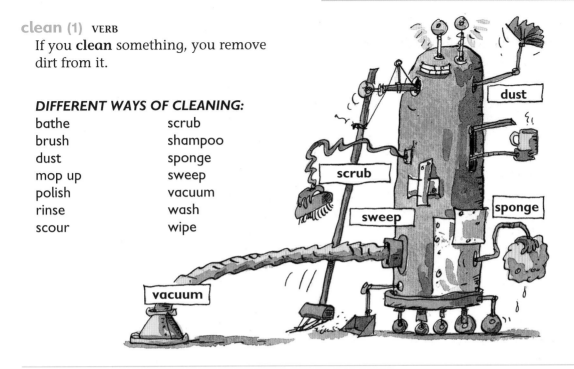

clean (2) ADJECTIVE

If something is **clean**, it is free from dirt.

blank
*She took a **blank** sheet and began to write.*

sparkling
*Penelope polished the glasses until they were **sparkling**.*

spotless
*The floor was **spotless** by the time they'd finished mopping it.*

clear (1) ADJECTIVE

If something you say or write is **clear**, it is easy to understand.

evident
*It was **evident** she didn't like me.*

obvious
*It was **obvious** from the first sentence that this was a sad book.*

plain
*"I'll make my idea **plain**, in words of one syllable," his brother said.*

simple
*The instructions were really **simple** and easy to follow.*

clear (2) ADJECTIVE

On a **clear** day there are no clouds in the sky.

bright
*On a **bright** day there are strong shadows on the ground.*

cloudless
*After the storm the sun shone brightly in the **cloudless** sky.*

fine
*"If the weather's **fine** we'll go to the beach tomorrow," said Dad.*

sunny
*It was **sunny** one minute and raining heavily the next.*

clear (3) ADJECTIVE

If a space is **clear**, there is nothing in it or it is free from things you don't want.

bare
*The room was **bare** when we got it ready for decorating.*

empty
*For once, the car park was **empty** and Mum could park close to the shops.*

clever ADJECTIVE

Someone who is **clever** can learn and understand things easily.

brainy
*Matt is really **brainy**. He gets top marks for everything.*

bright
*The baby's very **bright**. She's saying lots of words already.*

crafty
*A **crafty** old fox sneaked into the kitchen and stole the sausages.*

cunning
*She disguised her scar with a **cunning** use of make-up.*

gifted
*Kamal is a **gifted** writer.*

intelligent
*Our cat's quite **intelligent**. It understands ten words.*

inventive
*Matt was really **inventive** when it came to making up excuses.*

sharp
*That old man is still as **sharp** as ever.*

skilful
*Finches are **skilful** at getting the shells off sunflower seeds.*

talented
*He was a **talented** musician who could play any instrument well.*

climb VERB

When you **climb** something, you move upwards.

ascend
*The lift **ascended** so rapidly it took their breath away.*

clamber
*They **clambered** up the steep hill, clutching at bushes.*

shin up
*He **shinned up** a tree and looked through his telescope.*

clothes PLURAL NOUN

Clothes are the things people wear, such as shirts, trousers and dresses.

clothing
*You'll need warm **clothing** if you want to watch the fireworks.*

costume
*The actors in the film wore wonderful bright **costumes**.*

dress
*We were asked to wear informal **dress** to the dance.*

garments
*The charity shop is always glad of **garments** we no longer need.*

gear
*Sebastian had to have all the right **gear** for skateboarding.*

outfit
*Mum said her new **outfit** would be perfect for the wedding.*

wardrobe
*A famous designer planned the **wardrobe** for the musical.*

wear
*The shop sold everything you could want in the way of outdoor **wear**.*

cold ADJECTIVE

If the weather is **cold**, the temperature outside is low.

WORDS THAT DESCRIBE THE COLD:

arctic	frozen
biting	icy
bitter	raw
chilly	wintry
cool	
freezing	
frosty	

collect VERB

If you **collect** a number of things, you bring them together.

assemble
They assembled lots of food for the midnight feast.

gather
We went out to gather blackberries from a field near our house.

hoard
David hoarded empty glass bottles for his display.

raise
The school is trying to raise money for Children In Need.

save
We have been asked to save used stamps for a school project.

collection NOUN

A **collection** is a group of things brought together over a period of time.

assortment
The bathroom shelf is full of an assortment of shampoo bottles.

heap
Now and again, Dad adds another book to the heap.

mass
Dan worked his way through a mass of clothes to find his jeans.

pile
There was a pile of smelly old trainers in the corner.

set
"One more card and I'll have a complete set," said Raymond.

colour

colour NOUN

The **colour** of something is the way it looks in daylight.

shade
The walls were painted in different shades.

tint
The autumn leaves were taking on a warm red tint.

DIFFERENT COLOURS:

 black

 blue
navy
sky blue
turquoise

 brown
chocolate
coffee
fawn

 green
bottle-green
lime

 orange
tan

 pink
rose

 purple
lavender
lilac
mauve

 red
crimson
scarlet
vermilion

 white
cream
ivory

 yellow
amber
gold

come VERB

To **come** to a place is to move there or arrive there.

appear
We all giggled when the magician's rabbit appeared on stage.

approach
The guard dog growled loudly when the stranger approached.

arrive
The train arrived, and Grandma got out.

draw near
As they drew near to the castle, the great door opened.

show up
Most of the acts were good, but the conjuror didn't show up.

turn up
"Don't worry about us. We'll turn up later," said Ted.

visit
The Mayor is going to visit this afternoon.

ANTONYM: go

comfortable (1) ADJECTIVE

Something **comfortable** makes you feel relaxed and snug.

cosy
My room's warm and cosy in winter, even when it's freezing outside.

snug
Jamil felt snug tucked up in bed.

soft
Charlotte snuggled into the soft pillow and fell asleep straight away.

comfortable (2) ADJECTIVE

If you are **comfortable**, you feel at ease.

contented
The cat looked contented stretching out beside the fire.

happy
He was happy in his new room.

relaxed
Rebecca felt relaxed in the company of her friends.

ANTONYM: uncomfortable

common ADJECTIVE

If something is **common**, you often see it or it often happens.

average
It's average behaviour for a boy of his age.

everyday
Children feeding ducks on the pond is an everyday sight in this park.

standard
Power steering is standard in many cars that are made today.

usual
It is quite usual to see dogs and cats getting on well together.

competition NOUN

A **competition** is an event to see who is best at doing something.

championship
Our school is taking part in the junior swimming championship.

contest
There was a fierce contest between the red and blue teams.

game
Supporters cheered when their team won the game.

race
Attilio was by far the fastest runner and easily won the race.

tournament
My brother is through to the finals of the table-tennis tournament.

complete (1) ADJECTIVE

If something is **complete**, there is nothing missing.

entire
I've got the entire set of famous people in my album.

full
The teacher wanted a full report of the science experiment.

whole
Amy recited the whole poem without a single mistake.

complete (2) VERB

If you **complete** something, you finish it.

conclude
The head teacher concluded his lecture with a warning about litter.

do
Have you done your homework?

end
Simon ended his talk by asking if there were any questions.

finish
Charles couldn't think how to finish his story.

conversation NOUN

If you have a **conversation** with someone, you talk to each other.

chat
My mum likes to have a chat with friends over a cup of coffee.

discussion
There was a long discussion about which class Sheena should be put in.

gossip
The opening of the new school provided plenty of gossip.

talk
"I think we should have a talk about this," said his teacher.

cook

cook VERB

When you **cook** food, you prepare it for eating by heating it.

WAYS OF COOKING:
bake
barbecue
boil
fry
grill
microwave
poach
roast
steam
stew
stir-fry
toast

copy (1) NOUN

A **copy** is something made to look like something else.

fake
*The police say that painting is a **fake**.*

forgery
*He thought the man gave him a twenty-pound note, but it was a **forgery**.*

imitation
*Those jewels are only **imitations**. They're made of glass.*

photocopy
*"Can you give me a **photocopy** of that page?" asked Domenica.*

print
*It's not an original painting. It's a **print**.*

replica
*Manuel bought a plastic **replica** of the Eiffel Tower.*

copy (2) VERB

If you **copy** what someone does, you do the same thing.

follow
*"You must **follow** my movements exactly," said the dance teacher.*

imitate
*She can **imitate** her mum's voice.*

impersonate
*Frank is really good at **impersonating** famous people.*

mimic
*Ben can **mimic** the sounds animals make.*

mirror
*We carefully **mirrored** the movements of the karate teacher.*

trace
*Kim carefully **traced** the outline of the country into her book.*

correct ADJECTIVE

Something that is **correct** is true and has no mistakes.

accurate
*Make sure that your measurements are **accurate**, or the pieces will not fit together.*

exact
*It's no good guessing the amount of flour you need, it must be **exact**.*

precise
*"It's very important that the details you give are **precise**," said the policeman.*

right
*In the test, all his answers were **right**.*

true
*"Your report may be exciting," said her teacher, "but is it **true**?"*

cosy ADJECTIVE

A house or room that is **cosy** is comfortable and warm and not too big.

comfortable
*It was a **comfortable** room with lots of deep armchairs and thick rugs.*

snug
*We love our house because it's so **snug**.*

warm
*The fire sent out a **warm**, welcoming glow.*

count VERB

If you **count** a number of things, you find out how many there are.

add up
*She **added up** her pocket money to see if there was enough to go to the cinema.*

calculate
*Patrick **calculated** the number of hours he had spent doing his homework.*

tally
*The whole class stayed to **tally** the votes for the football captain.*

work out
***Work out** how much you've got, and how much more you need to buy this bike.*

cover VERB

If you **cover** something, you put something else over it to protect or hide it.

cloak
*Mist **cloaked** the mountain top, making it too dangerous to climb.*

conceal
*The boy **concealed** his work with his hand.*

hide
*During winter a blanket of snow **hid** the lawn and flowerbeds.*

mask
*Edmund **masked** his feeling of dismay with a smile.*

crack NOUN

A **crack** is a line or gap on something that shows it is damaged.

crevice
*Many spiders lurked in **crevices** in the old stone wall.*

gap
*They had to watch the game through a **gap** in the fence.*

split
*One of the pieces of wood had a large **split** at the end.*

crash NOUN

A **crash** is a sudden loud noise like something breaking.

clash
*Fabian brought the cymbals together with a **clash**.*

clatter
*The metal tray dropped to the ground with a **clatter**.*

smash
*There was a **smash** as the tea things hit the floor.*

crime

crime NOUN

A **crime** is something that is against the law of a country.

KINDS OF CRIMES:

arson	mugging	smuggling
burglary	murder	stealing
graffiti	piracy	terrorism
hijacking	robbery	theft
joyriding	shoplifting	vandalism

criminal NOUN

A **criminal** is someone who has done something that is against the law.

KINDS OF CRIMINALS:

arsonist	murderer	terrorist
burglar	pirate	thief
graffitist	robber	vandal
hijacker	shoplifter	
joyrider	smuggler	
mugger		

crooked ADJECTIVE

Something that is **crooked** is bent or twisted.

bent
*Shadha complained she couldn't get any juice through the **bent** straw, so the waiter got her another.*

twisting
*A **twisting** path led through the woods to the cottage.*

warped
*The wood was so **warped** they couldn't use it for anything but firewood.*

cross ADJECTIVE

Someone who is **cross** is angry about something.

angry
*Adrian was so **angry** he could hardly speak to her.*

annoyed
*Grandpa was **annoyed** when he found slugs had eaten his lettuces.*

grumpy
*Steven felt **grumpy** about not being well enough to go out.*

irritable
*Flies pestered the pony and made him very **irritable**.*

cruel ADJECTIVE

Someone who is **cruel** hurts people or animals without caring.

brutal
*The police said it was a **brutal** murder.*

cold-hearted
*The kidnapper was **cold-hearted** and ignored their pleas.*

heartless
*A **heartless** burglar smashed my grandma's favourite vase.*

vicious
*The burglar aimed a **vicious** kick at the guard dog.*

ANTONYM: kind

crush VERB

To **crush** something is to destroy its shape by squeezing it.

flatten
*They **flattened** the soft drink cans before recycling them.*

screw up
*Tibbles **screwed up** Mum's jacket when she slept on it.*

squash
*I dropped the shopping bag and **squashed** the tomatoes.*

cry (1) VERB

To **cry** means to call out loudly.

call

*He **called**, "Anybody there?"*

shout

*"I can't hear you," she **shouted**.*

shriek

*"Oh no!" **shrieked** Libby. "My new jeans have shrunk."*

yell

*Debbie had to **yell** above the din in the school playground.*

cry (2) VERB

When you **cry**, tears come from your eyes and trickle down your face.

grizzle

*The baby **grizzles** when he's hungry.*

howl

*My sister **howled** when her gerbil died.*

snivel

*"It's no good **snivelling**," said the ugly sisters. "You're not going to the ball."*

sob

*Tommy **sobbed** when he dropped his ice cream.*

wail

*"I wanted to go to the pantomime!" **wailed** Roly.*

weep

*Lara **wept** as she waved goodbye.*

whimper

*The puppy **whimpered** when Abdul went off to school.*

cut (1) VERB

If you **cut** something, you use a knife or scissors to remove parts of it.

carve

*Nicholas **carved** the wood into the shape of a cat.*

chop

*The cook **chopped** an onion and carrot into small pieces.*

clip

*Katherine **clipped** out an advertisement from the newspaper.*

mow

*Grandpa loves **mowing** his lawn to keep it neat and tidy.*

prune

*Rose bushes need **pruning** in spring.*

saw

*The gardener **sawed** up some wood to make a nesting box.*

slice

*Mrs Cratchit always **sliced** the bread too thinly.*

snip

*The hairdresser **snipped** off my long hair.*

trim

*The barber carefully **trimmed** the wizard's long beard.*

cut (2) VERB

To **cut** can mean to reduce something.

lower

*The supermarket is **lowering** a lot of its prices this week.*

reduce

*The government is trying to **reduce** the amount of traffic on the roads.*

a
b
Cc
d
e
f
g
h
i
j
k
l
m
n
o
p
q
r
s
t
u
v
w
x
y
z

Dd

damage VERB

To **damage** something means to harm or spoil it.

break
*My little sister has **broken** her doll already.*

chip
*Melanie was furious when she **chipped** her nail varnish.*

dent
*A gatepost got in the way and **dented** Dad's bumper.*

destroy
*An unexpected storm **destroyed** their beach hut.*

ruin
*"You've **ruined** my painting!" David screamed angrily.*

scratch
*Natalie's bike was **scratched** when it fell in the holly bush.*

spoil
*The baby knocked over a cup and **spoiled** my homework.*

vandalize
*Someone has **vandalized** the phone box on the corner of our street.*

wreck
*Rocks often **wreck** boats that come too close to shore.*

dance VERB

When you **dance**, you move your body in time to music.

SOME KINDS OF DANCING:
ballet dancing
ballroom dancing:
  foxtrot
  quickstep
  tango
  waltz
break dancing
disco dancing
folk dancing
Highland dancing
Irish dancing
line dancing
salsa
square dancing
tap dancing

ballroom dancing

ballet dancing

break dancing

Irish dancing

disco dancing

tap dancing

dangerous ADJECTIVE

If something is **dangerous**, it is likely to harm you.

alarming
*Rainforests are disappearing at an **alarming** rate.*

deadly
*The bite of some snakes can be **deadly**.*

harmful
*Medicines can be **harmful** if taken by the wrong person.*

menacing
*The captain waved his hook at Peter in a **menacing** fashion.*

risky
*They decided the adventure was getting too **risky**.*

treacherous
*Road conditions were **treacherous** in the thick fog.*

unsafe
*The bridge was rotten and **unsafe** to cross.*

ANTONYM: safe

dark ADJECTIVE

When it is **dark**, there is not enough light to see properly.

black
*The night was **black** and stormy.*

dim
*They could hardly see in the **dim** hallway.*

gloomy
*Rooms in the old castle were damp and **gloomy**.*

murky
*The submarine moved slowly in the **murky** depths of the ocean.*

shadowy
*A **shadowy** figure emerged from the misty woods.*

unlit
*It looked as if no one was home as all the rooms were **unlit**.*

delicious ADJECTIVE

Food that is **delicious** tastes or smells very nice.

mouthwatering
*At the village fair, the smell of frying onions was **mouthwatering**.*

scrumptious INFORMAL
*When we got home from school, Mum made us a **scrumptious** apple pie.*

tasty
*Andrew enjoyed a **tasty** snack on his way home from football training.*

ANTONYM: horrible

demonstrate (1) VERB

If someone **demonstrates** something, they show you how to do it.

explain
*Jamie **explained** how to separate the yolks and whites of eggs.*

illustrate
*Our music teacher **illustrated** how to play the violin.*

demonstrate (2) VERB

If people **demonstrate**, they hold a public meeting or march to show they are strongly for or against something.

march
*Sometimes thousands of people **march** in the capital to make their feelings known to the government.*

protest
*When people **protest**, they often meet to carry banners and shout slogans.*

deserted

deserted ADJECTIVE

If a place is **deserted**, there are no people there.

abandoned

*In the middle of the wood, the boys came upon an **abandoned** cottage.*

empty

*They saw a farmhouse and ran towards it to ask for water, but it was **empty**.*

destroy VERB

To **destroy** something means to damage it so much it cannot be mended.

crush

*The cottages were **crushed** under the feet of the angry giant.*

damage

*A tree fell in the storm and **damaged** our garden shed.*

demolish

*Builders **demolished** an empty house to make space for a new theatre.*

ruin

*People complained that the new building **ruined** their view.*

smash

*The jetty was **smashed** when a motorboat went out of control.*

wreck

*Many ships used to be **wrecked** on rocks around the coast before lighthouses were built to signal warnings.*

different (1) ADJECTIVE

Something that is **different** from something else is not like it in one or more ways.

assorted

*I like boxes of **assorted** biscuits best.*

changed

*He seemed **changed** somehow. Perhaps it was the short hair.*

mixed

*Alex had **mixed** feelings about going up a grade at school.*

opposite

*Mum's quite **opposite** to me. She likes my room to be tidy and I like it to be a mess.*

various

*He had **various** excuses for being late.*

different (2) ADJECTIVE

Something **different** is unusual and out of the ordinary.

bizarre

*Have you seen Polly's new hairstyle? It's really **bizarre**!*

extraordinary

*The magician at the party performed some **extraordinary** tricks.*

peculiar

*There was something **peculiar** about the expression on his face.*

special

*I wanted to do something **special** for my seventh birthday.*

unusual

*The baby had an **unusual** cry.*

→ something else

dig VERB

When people or animals **dig**, they break up a surface.

burrow

*Rabbits keep **burrowing** holes in the vegetable patch.*

excavate

*Archeologists are **excavating** at an ancient burial site.*

hollow

***Hollow** out the centre of the pumpkin and cut teeth and eyeholes in the skin.*

quarry

*Marble has been **quarried** in Italy for many centuries.*

scoop

*Libby **scooped** out some ice cream from the tub.*

tunnel

*Some prisoners of war **tunnelled** their way out of the camp.*

dirty ADJECTIVE

Something that is **dirty** is marked or covered with mud or stains.

filthy

*"Your hands are **filthy**," said Dad. "Go and wash them."*

foul

*The pigsty was **foul** with droppings, old straw and mud.*

greasy

*"I hate washing up **greasy** dishes," complained Simon.*

grimy

*Driving in the open-top car was great fun, but it made their faces pretty **grimy**.*

grubby

*He scrubbed at his knees with a **grubby** old tissue.*

messy

*Cleaning out the hamster is a **messy** job.*

muddy

*He came in from football with **muddy** shorts and boots.*

polluted

*The city air is **polluted** with vehicle fumes.*

stained

*Their clothes and mouths were **stained** with blackberry juice.*

untidy

*Litter blew around the park and made it look **untidy**.*

discover VERB

When you **discover** something, you find it or find out about it.

find

*My brother has **found** a good way to train the new puppy.*

uncover

*Mehmet lifted some papers and **uncovered** a book he'd thought was lost.*

unearth

*Kylie was digging a hole in the garden and **unearthed** an old pot.*

ANTONYM: hide

disguise

disguise VERB

If you **disguise** something, you change it so that people do not recognize it.

camouflage
The army camouflages tanks to hide them from aircraft.

conceal
She tried to conceal the spot on her chin.

cover
He covered his hair with a black wig.

dress up
"Is that your dad dressed up as Father Christmas?" asked Lucy.

mask
Dark sunglasses masked the expression in his eyes.

disturb (1) VERB

If you **disturb** someone, you interrupt them or spoil their peace and quiet.

bother
Don't bother me now, I'm busy.

hassle INFORMAL
"Quit hassling me, will you?" yelled my older sister.

interrupt
We're not allowed to interrupt Dad when he's working.

pester
Thomas pestered his brother in the library.

trouble
I don't want to trouble her now. She's watching her favourite programme.

disturb (2) VERB

If something **disturbs** you, it upsets or worries you.

alarm
I don't want to alarm you, but I think we should leave.

distress
The violence in the film distressed him.

frighten
The mouse was frightened when the cat sat by the cage.

upset
The noise upset the baby.

worry
Don't tell Grandma about the problem. It'll only worry her.

do (1) VERB

If you **do** something, you get on and finish it.

arrange
Dad is going to arrange everything.

carry out
The mechanic said he would carry out the repairs while we waited.

complete
"We should complete the work before the end of the week," said the builder.

cope with
Rachel's not sure she can cope with the decorations on her own.

finish
"You'll have to finish your homework before you go swimming," said Mum.

learn
What are you learning at the moment?

perform
Watch the clown perform his amazing juggling act.

do (2) VERB

If you say that something will **do**, you mean it is good enough.

be enough
*I wonder if half a page about my holidays will **be enough**?*

be sufficient
*I really hope this food will **be sufficient** for six people.*

be suitable
*Mum wanted to know if jeans would **be suitable** for the parents' evening.*

work
*They thought string might **work** as they didn't have any tape.*

drag VERB

If you **drag** a heavy object, you pull it along the ground.

draw
*The horse plodded on, **drawing** the heavy cart behind it.*

haul
*Fishermen **hauled** in their nets and found they had a large catch.*

pull
*Indigo **pulled** her friend from the river and rang for an ambulance.*

tow
*The farmer used a tractor to **tow** anything heavy around the farm.*

tug
*The boys **tugged** the sack of grain across the barn floor.*

draw (1) VERB

When you **draw**, you use something like a pencil or crayon to make a picture or a pattern.

doodle
*Holly **doodled** in her notebook as she listened to the teacher.*

paint
*I wanted to **paint** some pictures while I was on holiday.*

sketch
*In the field, an artist sat on a low stool **sketching** the scene.*

trace
*For homework we had to **trace** the outline of a map and fill in the rivers.*

draw (2) NOUN

A **draw** is the result in a game or competition in which nobody wins.

dead heat
*The result of the 100 metres sprint was a **dead heat**.*

tie
*Floella had hoped to win the competition, but there was a **tie** for first place.*

draw (3) VERB

If something **draws** you, it is so interesting that you move towards it.

attract
*A skydiving display **attracted** large crowds to the event.*

bring in
*We are hoping the advertising will **bring in** plenty of people.*

entice
*We were **enticed** into the shop by the display of cakes in the window.*

lure
*The witch **lured** the children into her house with promises of sweets.*

pull in
*The new programme has **pulled in** a lot of young viewers.*

dreadful ADJECTIVE

Something that is **dreadful** is very bad or unpleasant.

alarming
*Our test results were pretty **alarming**.*

awful
*I was off school with an **awful** cold.*

dire
*The teacher issued **dire** warnings about the standard of our homework.*

frightening
*The force of the storm was **frightening**.*

frightful
*After the halloween party the house was in a **frightful** mess.*

ghastly
*A **ghastly** wail echoed round the castle.*

horrible
*The jumper I got for my birthday was a **horrible** yellow colour.*

dream NOUN

A **dream** is something you want very much.

ambition
*It's Michael's **ambition** to be a pilot.*

daydream
*My favourite **daydream** is being interviewed on TV about my book.*

fantasy
*Chelsea has this **fantasy** about being a famous model.*

→ vision

drink VERB

When you **drink**, you take liquid into your mouth and swallow it.

gulp
*Boris was so thirsty he **gulped** down all his lemonade.*

guzzle
*"Don't **guzzle** like that. Drink it slowly," said Granny.*

lap
*Tigger **lapped** up the milk Simon put down for him.*

sip
*Julia **sipped** the hot tea carefully.*

slurp
*Augustus greedily **slurped** the chocolate milk shake.*

swallow
*She **swallowed** the medicine without tasting it.*

swig
*They **swigged** cola from the bottle.*

DIFFERENT THINGS TO DRINK:

cold drinks	hot drinks
cola	cocoa
fizz	coffee
fruit juice	hot chocolate
lemonade	hot milk
milk	malted milk
milk shake	tea
smoothie	
soya milk	
squash	
water	

tea

lemonade

cola

milk

fruit juice

drive   VERB

To **drive** means to make something or somebody go.

control
*Sharon **controlled** her car skilfully on the sandy beach.*

force
*The cruel baron **forced** the villagers from their cottages.*

push
*People at the front of the crowd were **pushed** forward.*

send
*Tom **sent** the ball over the fence.*

steer
*Rashid **steered** the go-kart into the side of the track.*

urge
*The knight **urged** his horse to a full gallop.*

dry   ADJECTIVE

Something that is **dry** has no water in it at all.

arid
*Large areas of Mexico are **arid** desert.*

barren
*No crops could grow on the **barren** land.*

parched
*The garden was **parched** and all the seedlings died.*

dull (1)   ADJECTIVE

Something that is **dull** is not interesting.

boring
*It was the most **boring** action film they'd ever seen.*

dreary
*I spent a **dreary** morning being dragged round the shops.*

tedious
*John found his cousin's story **tedious**.*

dull (2)   ADJECTIVE

Something that is **dull** is not bright or clear.

cloudy
*The day was so **cloudy** we thought it might rain at any moment.*

dismal
*A most surprising thing happened on that **dismal** wintry afternoon.*

drab
*She wore a **drab** grey dress and grimy brown shoes.*

gloomy
*It was difficult to see the ogre in the **gloomy** light of the cave.*

grey
*The ugly duckling was a **grey** colour before he turned into a beautiful swan.*

miserable
*I like playing board games on **miserable**, rainy days.*

ANTONYM: bright

Ee

a
b
c
d
Ee
f
g
h
i
j
k
l
m
n
o
p
q
r
s
t
u
v
w
x
y
z

eager   ADJECTIVE

If you are **eager**, you very much want to do or have something.

enthusiastic
*There were plenty of **enthusiastic** volunteers to help plan the school garden.*

impatient
*Mark was **impatient** to get back to school after the holidays.*

keen
*Brownie was **keen** to enter the competition at the dog show.*

longing
*Rachel was **longing** to see her newborn baby brother.*

easy   ADJECTIVE

Something that is **easy** can be done without difficulty.

clear
*The way the teacher showed us made everything **clear**.*

obvious
*The answer to the problem was **obvious**. I gave Tom some of my ice cream and he stopped crying.*

plain
*It was **plain** to see he didn't like spiders.*

simple
*"Shelling the peas shouldn't take you long," said Mum. "It's a **simple** job."*

ANTONYM: difficult

eat   VERB

When you **eat**, you chew and swallow food.

bite
*"**Bite** the jammy bit of the doughnut first," said Isaac.*

chew
*Cows **chew** the grass thoughtfully.*

devour
*They **devour** the sandwiches as fast as she makes them.*

gnaw
*Boggart happily lay down in the garden and **gnawed** his bone.*

gobble
*Mum told them to stop **gobbling** sweets.*

graze
*Sheep **graze** in the meadow until the farmer brings them in for the night.*

have a meal
*"We **have a meal** together every evening," said Mum.*

munch
*The horse likes to **munch** apples, carrots and oats.*

nibble
*Kylie **nibbles** her food like a mouse.*

peck
*Pigeons **peck** seeds and breadcrumbs thrown by the tourists.*

swallow
*Arthur was too busy talking to **swallow** his food properly.*

edge NOUN

An **edge** is the end or side of something.

border
*Her wallpaper had a **border** with animals on it.*

boundary
*The farmer planted a hedge along the **boundary** of his land.*

brim
*He filled his glass up to the **brim**.*

margin
*There were holes in the **margin** of the paper to fit the folder.*

rim
*They stood at the **rim** of the crater and gazed down into the depths.*

effort NOUN

Effort is the energy needed to do something.

energy
*It took a huge amount of **energy** to climb to the top of the hill.*

force
*With great **force**, the giant pushed a boulder from the mouth of the cave.*

struggle
*The boys found it a **struggle** to drag the heavy sack.*

work
*"They have put a lot of **work** into this project," said the teacher.*

empty (1) ADJECTIVE

Something that is **empty** has no people or things in it.

bare
*John's room was **bare** apart from a few packing cases.*

blank
*Hasan stared at the **blank** pages of his old diary.*

clear
*The road was **clear** and we arrived in record time.*

deserted
*We knocked on the door, but the place was completely **deserted**.*

unoccupied
*The house had been **unoccupied** for years.*

vacant
*We had a job to find a **vacant** field for our picnic.*

ANTONYM: full

empty (2) VERB

If you **empty** a container, you pour or take everything out of it.

clear out
*Dad started to **clear out** the shed today.*

drain
*There was a hole in his bucket and the water **drained** out.*

unload
*The children helped **unload** the car when they got home.*

ANTONYM: fill

Ee

encourage

a
b
c
d

Ee

f
g
h
i
j
k
l
m
n
o
p
q
r
s
t
u
v
w
x
y
z

encourage (1) VERB

If you **encourage** someone, you tell them that what they are doing is good.

cheer
However tired they get, the news they are winning always **cheers** them.

console
Jake finds drawing hard, but his teacher **consoles** him and he goes on trying.

reassure
Our dog is nervous of the water, and we have to **reassure** him.

encourage (2) VERB

To **encourage** something means to support it.

aid
Rain and sunshine **aid** the growth of plants in the garden.

help
My mum comes into school to **help** the little ones to read.

support
The head teacher **supports** our efforts to raise money for Children In Need.

end (1) NOUN

The **end** of a period of time or an event is the last part.

conclusion
The governors' meeting was brought to a swift **conclusion**.

ending
The **ending** of the story made me cry.

finish
Patrick was watching the match but he missed the **finish**.

ANTONYM: beginning

end (2) NOUN

The **end** of something is the furthest point of it.

back
Most damage was to the **back** of the bus.

point
The **point** of his pencil was always sharp.

rear
People in the **rear** carriage of the train were squashed together.

tip
Our cat shows her anger by twitching the **tip** of her tail.

end (3) VERB

If something **ends**, it finishes.

break up
School **breaks up** next week.

conclude
The minister **concluded** his speech by thanking his team.

finish
Luckily the play **finished** in time for us to catch the bus.

stop
Work **stopped** suddenly when the fire alarm sounded.

entertain VERB

If you **entertain** somebody, you do something they enjoy and find amusing.

amuse
Our baby is very easy to **amuse**, unless he's hungry or tired.

delight
The conjuror **delighted** everybody with his magical tricks.

occupy
Can you think of something to **occupy** the children while they are waiting?

please
She made a list of party games that would **please** her friends.

escape VERB

If a person or animal **escapes**, they get away from whatever is holding them.

bolt
The horse **bolted** before they could shut the stable door.

break free
The cage was locked but the hamster still managed to **break free**.

get away
She kept me talking and it was ages before I could **get away**.

run away
The police officer tried to make an arrest but the thief **ran away**.

run off
We tried to hang on to the stray dog but it **ran off**.

even (1) ADJECTIVE

If something is **even**, it is flat and level.

flat
The path was nice and **flat**.

level
They set up their football pitch on a **level** bit of ground.

smooth
The ice was **smooth** enough to skate on.

even (2) ADJECTIVE

If a contest is **even**, the two sides have the same chance of winning.

equal
The twins had an **equal** chance of winning the race.

level
The scores were **level** at half time.

→ neck and neck

excitement NOUN

Excitement is feeling happy and unable to rest.

action
I love the **action** of an adventure holiday.

activity
There was plenty of **activity** going on in the games room.

commotion
We went to see what the **commotion** was all about.

thrills
They went on all the fairground rides in search of **thrills**.

extraordinary ADJECTIVE

Someone or something that is **extraordinary** is very special or unusual.

amazing
Ranjit came to the party wearing the most **amazing** gear.

bizarre
Her behaviour was totally **bizarre**.

odd
"That's an **odd** sight," said Mum. "Daffodils in August!"

strange
The magician's cloak was covered in **strange** designs.

unusual
It's **unusual** to see a kangaroo in a supermarket.

→ out of this world

ANTONYM: **ordinary**

Ff

fade VERB

If something such as light, colour or sound **fades**, it becomes less strong.

bleach

"Be careful drying your jeans outside," said Granny. "The sun might **bleach** them."

die away

The sound of clapping **died away**.

grow dim

Light in the room **grew dim**.

vanish

The buzzing noise **vanished** as soon as we stepped outside.

fail (1) VERB

If someone **fails** when they try to do something, they cannot do it.

be defeated

Nina hoped to win enough votes to be captain, but she **was defeated**.

be in vain

Robin's efforts to score a winning goal **were in vain**.

be unsuccessful

The head teacher's advertisement for more staff **was unsuccessful**.

ANTONYM: succeed

fail (2) VERB

If something **fails**, it stops working or does not work so well.

give out

Just when they needed it most, the washing machine **gave out**.

sink

When Gunnar realized he wasn't dreaming, his courage began to **sink**.

stop working

The computer **stopped working** and they couldn't print out their stories.

faint ADJECTIVE

Something like a sound or mark that is **faint** is not easy to hear or see.

dim

Light from the torch grew **dim** as the batteries failed.

faded

After several washes, lettering on the T-shirt became **faded**.

indistinct

They heard the sound of a voice but it was too **indistinct** to make out words.

low

Dark clouds filled the sky and there was a **low** rumble of thunder.

vague

He had a pleasant dream but it left only a **vague** memory.

ANTONYM: strong

fair (1) ADJECTIVE

Something that is **fair** seems reasonable to most people.

reasonable
"We get a reasonable amount of pocket money," said Anthony.

right
He's got a bigger piece than me. It's just not right!

ANTONYM: unfair

fair (2) ADJECTIVE

If someone's work is **fair**, it is about average.

average
His work is average, neither good nor bad.

not bad
This is not bad, but you can do better when you try.

satisfactory
His performance in the football match was satisfactory.

fair (3) ADJECTIVE

People who are **fair** have light-coloured hair or skin.

blond(e)
My friend, Fiona, has straight blonde hair. I wish I had straight hair, mine's very curly.

light
Dorothea's hair is long and brown with light streaks.

pale
His pale skin burns easily in the sun so he keeps it covered up.

fair (4) NOUN

A **fair** is an outdoor entertainment.

bazaar
Maria bought her shawl at a bazaar.

festival
Here's our float for the May Day festival.

fete
The school fete was a great success.

market
Mum buys fruit at the local market.

show
The tractor company did well at the country show.

faithful ADJECTIVE

If you are **faithful** to someone, you can be trusted and relied on.

devoted
His dog was so devoted to him that she refused to leave when he was ill.

loyal
My sister only tells her secrets to people she knows are loyal.

reliable
You can count on reliable friends never to let you down.

true
Max is a footballer who will always be true to his team.

trustworthy
She may have a lovely smile, but is she a trustworthy member of the club?

fall

fall (1) VERB

When someone or something **falls**, they drop towards the ground.

collapse
Everybody screamed and laughed when the tent collapsed.

crash
The sign came loose and then crashed to the ground.

crumple
She burst into tears and crumpled in a heap.

descend
The pilot escaped from his burning plane and descended safely to the ground.

dip
The road dipped suddenly and they hit a sheet of water.

drop
She screamed and the tray dropped with a clatter.

slip
The precious vase slipped from his hands.

stumble
Hansel and Gretel stumbled several times on the rough path.

trip
Josephine tripped over the kerb and banged her knee.

tumble
The baby tumbled over as he tried to walk.

→ come a cropper; drop like a stone

fall (2) VERB

To **fall** can mean to decrease in amount or value.

decrease
Numbers of children at the school have decreased this year.

drop
The temperature dropped to freezing.

go down
Dad says my pocket money will go down if I'm not careful.

→ plummet

ANTONYM: **rise**

false (1) ADJECTIVE

If something is **false**, it is not the real thing.

artificial
The actress wore an artificial smile.

bogus
He spoke with a bogus American accent.

fake
The bank robber tried to leave the country using a fake passport.

forged
The letter had a forged signature.

ANTONYM: **real**

false (2) ADJECTIVE

If something you say is **false**, it is not true.

incorrect
Some of the details given by the suspect were incorrect.

untrue
I think the reason you've given for not doing your homework is untrue.

wrong
Rumours about the supermarket closing down are wrong.

ANTONYM: **true**

fast (1) ADJECTIVE

Someone or something that is **fast** can move very quickly.

brisk
*Before lunch, Mum took us for a **brisk** walk in the park.*

express
*We got an **express** train to the city.*

high-speed
*I have a new **high-speed** computer.*

hurried
*After a **hurried** lunch we all went off to the cinema.*

quick
*The robbers managed a **quick** getaway.*

rapid
*The mouse made small, **rapid** movements.*

speedy
*When we saw Mum's face we made a **speedy** exit.*

swift
*With a **swift** action Jasmine leaped out of the car.*

➜ jet-propelled

ANTONYM: **slow**

fast (2) ADVERB

If you do something **fast**, you do it quickly and without delay.

quickly
*The Gingerbread Man ran away **quickly** from the baker.*

rapidly
*The family walked **rapidly** through the churchyard.*

swiftly
*Goddard moved **swiftly** and silently after his enemy.*

➜ in a flash; like a shot

ANTONYM: **slowly**

fast (3) ADVERB

If something is held **fast**, it is held firmly and strongly.

firmly
*The dog dragged Ben along, but he held **firmly** onto the lead.*

securely
*They tethered the goat **securely** to a post in the field.*

tightly
*Francesca held on **tightly** to the rabbit as its owner approached.*

a b c d e **Ff** g h i j k l m n o p q r s t u v w x y z

fear

fear NOUN

Fear is the nasty feeling you have when you think you are in danger.

alarm
*Dom froze in **alarm** as a huge dog approached her.*

dread
*They waited in **dread** for the arrival of Aunt Agatha.*

fright
*He yelped in **fright** as the door burst open.*

horror
Horror gripped Matt as the dark form loomed above him.

panic
*Jack flew from the room in **panic**.*

terror
*Becky stared at the ghost in **terror**.*

feel (1) VERB

If you **feel** an object, you touch it to find out what it is like.

handle
*The princess looked thoughtful as she **handled** the velvet.*

stroke
*May I **stroke** the kitten's fur?*

touch
*I didn't want to **touch** the cactus. It looked prickly.*

feel (2) VERB

If you **feel** something, like happy or sad, that is how you are at that time.

be aware of
*Peter **was aware of** a nagging worry at the back of his mind.*

experience
*She **experienced** a sudden sense of loss.*

notice
*Max **noticed** a warm, happy feeling creeping over him.*

feel (3) VERB

If you **feel** something is the case, you believe it.

believe
*If I practise my writing, I **believe** I may become a novelist one day.*

consider
*Mum **considered** one cake was enough.*

judge
*I **judged** the baby would cry if we played with her for too long.*

think
*Everyone **thought** Meera would be good in the team.*

fierce ADJECTIVE
Something that is **fierce** is dangerous.

aggressive
*Even pets can become **aggressive** if they have new babies.*

dangerous
*Many large wild animals are **dangerous**, even when they look relaxed.*

ferocious
*The tiger's **ferocious** snarl frightened the other animals.*

savage
*You only have to watch wildlife programmes to see how **savage** lions can be.*

ANTONYM: **gentle**

fight (1) VERB

If you **fight** someone, you try to hurt them.

battle

*Tweedledum and Tweedledee **battled** over a rattle.*

brawl

*Some men were **brawling** in the street.*

grapple

*The old lady **grappled** with a boy who tried to steal her handbag.*

struggle

*John and David **struggled** for possession of the cricket bat.*

fight (2) NOUN

A **fight** is a fierce struggle.

battle

*There are lots of **battles** during a war.*

duel

*The two men settled their quarrel with a **duel**.*

fight (3) NOUN

A **fight** can be an angry disagreement.

argument

*A fierce **argument** broke out about who broke the vase.*

dispute

*There was a **dispute** over whose foot would fit the glass slipper.*

row

*Last week my parents had a **row**.*

squabble

*It was only a small **squabble**. They were soon friends again.*

find (1) VERB

When you **find** someone or something you have been looking for, you see them.

come across

*He thought he would **come across** the book if he kept looking.*

notice

*I knew he would **notice** the bright purple envelope.*

see

*A shop assistant was first to **see** the lost little boy.*

spot

*We hoped to **spot** our friend at the cinema.*

trace

*My dad has been trying to **trace** his long-lost brother.*

track down

*The police would soon **track down** their main suspect.*

find (2) VERB

To **find** can mean to learn or realize something.

become aware of

*If the police **become aware of** the motive, they can solve the crime.*

discover

*The princess won't be able to sleep until she **discovers** the pea under her mattress.*

learn

*"You **learn**," said Jason, "that it's a bad idea to get on the wrong side of him."*

realize

*"When did you **realize** you'd lost your wallet?" asked the restaurant manager.*

fine

fine (1) ADJECTIVE

Something that is **fine** is extremely good.

beautiful
There was a **beautiful** view of the forest from the hotel window.

excellent
Julia tried very hard and produced an **excellent** piece of work.

magnificent
The gardens at the country house were really **magnificent**.

outstanding
The class gave an **outstanding** performance at the concert.

splendid
After the match, Uncle Albert gave us a **splendid** meal.

fine (2) ADJECTIVE

Fine can mean small in size or thickness.

delicate
The bride's veil was made of such a **delicate** material it hardly seemed to be there.

lightweight
Lightweight seeds from the dandelion heads blew across the garden.

powdery
Dust lay in a **powdery** film on every surface in the room.

thin
Spiders can produce perfect webs with **thin** threads.

finish VERB

When you **finish** something, you reach the end of it.

close
The piece of music **closed** with a roll of drums and a clash of cymbals.

complete
Sanjay **completed** his poem and read it out to his friends.

conclude
"I will **conclude** this talk," said the Mayor, "by thanking my staff."

end
Hannah's party **ended** with a colourful firework display.

stop
The test came to an end and the children **stopped** writing.

ANTONYM: **start**

firm (1) ADJECTIVE

Something that is **firm** does not move easily when you press or push it.

hard
This pear's not ripe. It's still **hard**.

rigid
The bodybuilder's muscles were **rigid**.

set
Now the glue is **set**, it should be okay.

firm (2) ADJECTIVE

Something that is **firm** does not shake or move.

secure
The engineer made sure the nuts and bolts were **secure**.

solid
The table was **solid** enough to climb on.

firm (3) ADJECTIVE

If someone is **firm**, they will not change their mind.

definite
*I can take that as a **definite** "no" then?*

strict
*One of our teachers at school is very **strict** about noise.*

unshakable
*The doctor has an **unshakable** belief in lots of exercise.*

fit (1) VERB

If something **fits** something else, it is right for it.

belong to
*This cap **belongs to** the green bottle.*

be suitable
*We wanted some shoes that **were suitable** for school.*

go with
*According to the instructions, this bit **goes with** that.*

match
*Joe needed a bit of jigsaw to **match** the edge pieces.*

fit (2) ADJECTIVE

Someone who is **fit** is healthy.

healthy
*Grandma's **healthier** than some people half her age.*

strong
*Calum's **strong** as an ox.*

well
*He's **well** enough to carry on training.*

fix (1) VERB

If you **fix** something somewhere, you put it there firmly.

attach
*A caterpillar **attaches** itself to a plant to spin its cocoon.*

fasten
*The suspect's wrists were **fastened** together with handcuffs.*

secure
*He **secured** his bike to the stand with a padlock and chain.*

stick
*Pat **stuck** a stamp on the envelope.*

fix (2) VERB

If you **fix** something that has broken, you make it work again.

mend
*I had to **mend** my model aircraft after it crashed.*

patch up
*We managed to **patch up** the airbed.*

repair
*Holly found someone who could **repair** her computer.*

flow VERB

If liquid **flows** in a certain direction, it moves there steadily.

cascade
*I forgot to turn off the tap and water **cascaded** all over the floor.*

flood
*The river broke its banks and **flooded** across the fields.*

leak
*We need a new tank. Water's **leaking** from the old one.*

pour
*Rain **poured** from the choked gutters and soaked the walls.*

spurt
*Blood **spurted** from his wound.*

flower

flower NOUN

A **flower** is the part of the plant that has coloured petals. When the petals fade, fruit or seeds develop.

WILD FLOWERS:

bluebell
buttercup
daisy
dandelion
foxglove
primrose

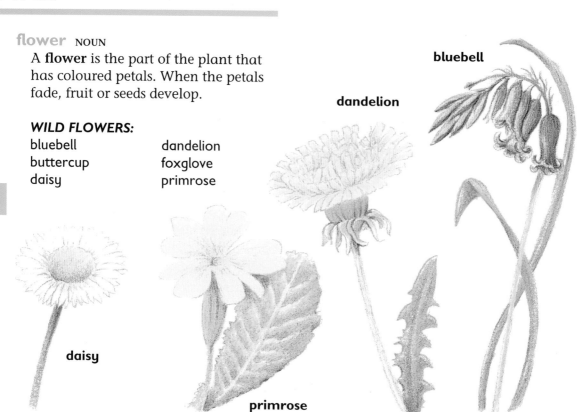

bluebell

dandelion

daisy

primrose

GARDEN FLOWERS:

chrysanthemum
crocus
daffodil
geranium
hollyhock
lily
pansy
rose
snowdrop
sunflower
tulip
violet
wallflower

sunflower

lily

daffodil

rose

fluffy ADJECTIVE

Something that is **fluffy** is very soft and light.

feathery
Snow fell in feathery flakes, white against the dark sky.

furry
Jamilla gently stroked the kitten's furry black coat.

light
Her angora jumper was wonderfully light and warm.

soft
The soft white bread was still warm from the oven.

fly VERB

When a bird, insect or aircraft **flies**, it moves through the air.

flutter
A butterfly fluttered towards a flower.

glide
An owl glides silently above the corn.

soar
The plane soars to about a thousand metres before it levels out.

swoop
We watched a hawk swoop down and rise again with something in its claws.

fold VERB

If you **fold** something, you bend it so that one part lies over another.

bend
He wrote on the envelope, "Photographs. Please do not bend."

crease
The instructions told him to crease along the dotted line.

crumple
Ben crumpled the note and put it away in his pocket.

tuck
Mum showed me how to tuck in the sheet.

follow (1) VERB

If you **follow** someone who is moving, you move along behind them.

chase
William chased me as far as the gate, then gave up.

pursue
The police pursued the suspect and soon caught him.

shadow
A detective shadowed her throughout the afternoon.

tail
We tailed him for hours, but lost him in the crowd.

track
The gamekeeper showed us the best way to track deer.

follow (2) VERB

If one thing **follows** another, it happens after it.

come after
Games usually come after lunch.

come next
We enjoyed the clowns and wondered what would come next.

follow (3) VERB

If you **follow** something such as an explanation, you understand it.

grasp
Hugh grasped the idea quite quickly when the teacher explained it.

realize
She finally realized what her dad was getting at.

take in
For a moment he could not take in what she was saying.

understand
The explanation was clear enough. I understood it at once.

→ get the picture

a
b
c
d
e
Ff
g
h
i
j
k
l
m
n
o
p
q
r
s
t
u
v
w
x
y
z

foolish

foolish ADJECTIVE

Something or somebody **foolish** is silly or unwise.

daft INFORMAL
*Emily said it would be **daft** to go out in that weather without a coat.*

idiotic
*He's always got some **idiotic** plan that is sure to go wrong.*

mad
*It was a **mad** idea, but we agreed it might just work.*

silly
*I don't like the **silly** things she does, so I'm not her friend any more.*

unwise
*Our cat is anxious about her new kittens and it's **unwise** to touch them.*

force NOUN

The **force** of something is the powerful effect it has.

impact
*With the **impact** of the storm, trees crashed and roofs were blown off.*

might
*They fought the battle with the **might** of two thousand soldiers.*

power
*The giant used all his **power** to uproot the tree.*

strength
*Slowly, the **strength** of the wind faded and they were able to leave their shelter.*

violence
*He was powerful, but he was against using **violence** to achieve his ends.*

fragile ADJECTIVE

Something that is **fragile** is easily broken or damaged.

breakable
*They wrapped all the **breakable** things in sheets of newspaper.*

brittle
*Fine china teacups are **brittle** and are not usually for every day.*

delicate
*My sister's wedding cake was covered in **delicate** sugar rosebuds.*

flimsy
*The framework of the tent was too **flimsy** and it collapsed.*

frail
*As he clambered into the **frail** boat, it rocked and almost threw him out.*

thin
*Oliver's legs looked **thin**, as if they would hardly bear his weight.*

fresh ADJECTIVE

If something feels **fresh**, it is clean, cool and refreshing.

bracing
*After lunch we needed a walk in the **bracing** sea air.*

clean
*Back home after camping, the best thing was to sleep in **clean** sheets.*

clear
*They breathed in the **clear** early morning air outside the cottage.*

pure
*We drank deeply of the **pure** water that bubbled up from the spring.*

friend NOUN

A **friend** is someone you know well and like very much.

ally
In a fight, it is as well to know who are your allies.

companion
The old lady's only companion was a large dog.

mate INFORMAL
Samuel can usually be found talking to his mates.

playmate
Meera's playmates waited for her to finish lunch.

friendly ADJECTIVE

If you are **friendly** to someone, you behave in a kind and pleasant way to them.

affectionate
The letter from Simon was affectionate, with kisses at the end.

amiable
There are lots of amiable people working at our supermarket.

close
Amy and her sister Rosie are very close and go everywhere together.

kind
I enjoy going to the dentist because she's so kind.

loving
Emma always gives her grandma a loving hug when they meet.

welcoming
Mrs Jones opened the front door and greeted them with a welcoming smile.

frighten VERB

If something **frightens** you, it makes you afraid.

alarm
Don't let that sound alarm you. It's only a ghost rattling its chains.

scare
The dog scared me when it snarled and moved forward.

shock
I was shocked when a bear stopped to talk to me.

startle
The sudden bang startled him.

terrify
Fireworks terrify our cat.

→ make your blood run cold; make your flesh creep

frightened ADJECTIVE

Someone who is **frightened** thinks that something nasty might happen.

afraid
Who's afraid of the big bad wolf?

alarmed
Ben was alarmed when he heard something tapping at the window.

scared
Miss Muffet was scared when a spider sat down beside her.

startled
The pony was startled when a paper bag blew across its path.

terrified
One of the new ducklings is terrified of water.

a
b
c
d
e
Ff
g
h
i
j
k
l
m
n
o
p
q
r
s
t
u
v
w
x
y
z

fruit

fruit NOUN

A **fruit** is the part of a plant that develops from the flower and contains the seeds. Many fruits are good to eat.

KINDS OF FRUITS:

apple	lemon	peach
avocado	lime	pear
banana	mango	pineapple
blueberry	melon	plum
cherry	orange	raspberry
grape	papaya	strawberry
grapefruit	passion fruit	tomato
kiwi fruit		

apple

bananas

grapes

lemon

kiwi fruits

mango

orange

pineapple

passion fruits

strawberries

full (1) ADJECTIVE

Full can mean leaving nothing out.

complete
*Marty has got a **complete** set of Harry Potter books.*

entire
*My dad has sold his **entire** collection of stamps.*

whole
*The teacher said she wanted to hear the **whole** story.*

full (2) ADJECTIVE

If something is **full**, there is no room for anything more.

brimming
*The glass of milk was **brimming**, so he lifted it carefully.*

bulging
*Jo's shopping bag was **bulging**.*

crammed
*The bus was **crammed** and Josh couldn't get on.*

crowded
*The cafe was **crowded**, so we went to the park instead.*

heaped
*She came back with a **heaped** plate.*

packed
*When we arrived, the hall was **packed**.*

fun NOUN

Fun is something enjoyable that makes you feel happy.

amusement
*They got a lot of **amusement** from watching the puppies play.*

enjoyment
*In Ratty's opinion, lots of **enjoyment** could be had messing about in boats.*

entertainment
*The best part of the **entertainment** was watching the tightrope walker.*

pleasure
*His idea of **pleasure** was sitting quietly on the beach.*

funny (1) ADJECTIVE

Funny people or things make you laugh.

amusing
*Grandma finds cartoons **amusing**.*

comical
*I liked the clown. Even his face was **comical**.*

hilarious
*David told us this **hilarious** story.*

humorous
*Mai Lin likes **humorous** books best.*

ridiculous
*His uncle wore a **ridiculous** green hat to the party.*

witty
*Our teacher often says **witty** things.*

funny (2) ADJECTIVE

Something that is **funny** is rather strange or surprising.

odd
*I had an **odd** feeling something was going to happen.*

peculiar
*When she woke up, Heather had a **peculiar** expression on her face.*

strange
*The old man was wearing **strange** clothes.*

unusual
*The house had an **unusual** name.*

weird
*He was very tall and thin, and was dressed in a **weird** cloak.*

a b c d e **Ff** g h i j k l m n o p q r s t u v w x y z

Gg

game NOUN

A **game** is something you play for sport or fun. Most games have rules.

amusement
What amusements have we got for the little ones?

competition
Claudette won first prize in the competition.

contest
There was an arm-wrestling contest and I won.

entertainment
The only available entertainment was snakes and ladders.

match
Our team is bound to win the football match this afternoon.

gap (1) NOUN

A **gap** is a space between two things, or a hole in something solid.

break
The sun shone brightly through a break in the clouds.

chink
Chinks were appearing in the old fence.

crack
Every room had cracks in the plaster.

hole
A rabbit had dug a hole under the fence.

space
They tried to find a space in the hedge to look through.

gap (2) NOUN

A **gap** is a period of time when you stop doing something.

interval
There was an interval of fifteen minutes after the first act.

lull
Jade waited for a lull in the conversation so that she could say something.

pause
There was a short pause before the head teacher spoke again.

gasp VERB

When you **gasp**, you take a short quick breath through your mouth.

breathe heavily
When they reached the top of the hill, they were breathing heavily.

choke
The firemen found a woman choking in the dense smoke.

pant
"Quick!" she panted. "I must have a drink of water."

puff
They puffed and groaned as they finished the race.

wheeze
Paul was wheezing and coughing because of his very bad cold.

gather (1) VERB

If people or animals **gather**, they come together in a group.

assemble

*Students were asked to **assemble** in the hall for a special announcement.*

crowd round

*A woman fell and passers-by **crowded round** to help or offer advice.*

flock

*He was such a good speaker, people would **flock** from miles around to hear him.*

meet

*Parties are wonderful places to **meet** and have fun.*

gather (2) VERB

If you **gather** things, you collect them from different places.

accumulate

*"I don't know how I've managed to **accumulate** all this rubbish," Mum said.*

bring together

*They were told to **bring together** all the things they could find beginning with the letter "B".*

collect

*In the autumn the children **collected** leaves of different colours.*

hoard

*My grandpa **hoards** things he's sure will come in useful one day.*

stockpile

*During a war, people often **stockpile** tins of food.*

gather (3) VERB

If you **gather** something, you learn or believe it.

believe

*I **believe** they're putting traffic lights on that dangerous corner at last.*

hear

*We **hear** there's going to be a new teacher next term.*

learn

*She **learned** that her cousin was getting married in the spring.*

understand

*I **understand** we're to have a new swimming pool.*

general ADJECTIVE

You use **general** to say that something is true in most cases.

accepted

*The **accepted** feeling is that pollution is a dangerous thing.*

broad

*You can often tell which TV programmes will have a **broad** appeal.*

common

*It is **common** knowledge that swimming is good for you.*

usual

*The **usual** behaviour of children at this school is very good.*

widespread

*There is a **widespread** understanding of the need to recycle.*

gentle

gentle ADJECTIVE

Someone who is **gentle** is kind, calm and sensitive.

calm
*Mum has a **calm** voice, even when she's feeling angry.*

kind
*The nurse who looked after me was very **kind**.*

soft-hearted
*Simon's a **soft-hearted** little boy. He would hate to upset anyone.*

tender
*She gazed at the baby with a **tender** smile.*

get (1) VERB

If you **get** something, you fetch it or are given it.

be given
*I hope I **am given** a bike for my birthday.*

bring
*They weren't sure what food to **bring** for the picnic.*

buy
*We didn't know what to **buy** Annabel for her birthday.*

collect
*Susan went to **collect** interesting shells from the beach.*

earn
*How much money do paper boys **earn**?*

fetch
*The dragon likes **fetching** our paper, but he always sets light to it.*

gather
*They went to **gather** wood for the fire.*

win
*He's not very good at sums, but he **wins** a prize for his poetry every year.*

get (2) VERB

Get often means the same as become or arrive.

arrive
*My brother **arrives** home in time for dinner most nights.*

become
*Evenings **become** darker much earlier in winter.*

come
*We reached the platform before the train **came** in.*

grow
*The sky was **growing** lighter as the sun came up.*

reach
*"Can you **reach** that tin on the top shelf, please?" asked Gran.*

turn
*The leaves are **turning** redder every day.*

ghost NOUN

A **ghost** is a shadowy figure of someone no longer living that some people believe they see.

phantom
*Ron gasped. "It's the **phantom** that haunts the castle!"*

spectre
*Hamlet saw the **spectre** of his dead father.*

spirit
*"I don't believe in **spirits**," Danny said.*

spook
*The boys went out **spook** hunting.*

gift NOUN

A **gift** is a present.

contribution
*Our teacher was collecting **contributions** for children in hospital.*

donation
*A **donation** from the parents helped the school buy more books.*

offering
*The primroses were only a small **offering** but Mum was really pleased.*

present
*Everyone brought a **present** when they came to the party.*

give VERB

If you **give** someone something, you hand it to them or provide it for them.

contribute
*Auntie Charlotte often **contributes** to animal charities.*

donate
*Several parents were able to **donate** prizes for the raffle.*

hand over
***Hand over** your mobile to the teacher before you go into class.*

offer
*She decided to **offer** me one of her sweets.*

present
*One of the school governors came to **present** a prize for swimming.*

provide
*The cat-rescue people asked us to **provide** tins of cat food.*

supply
*When it rains, my teacher always **supplies** drawing paper to the class.*

gloomy (1) ADJECTIVE

If a place is **gloomy**, it is dark and dull.

dark
*The room was **dark**, with cobwebs hanging down everywhere.*

dismal
*It was a **dismal** landscape with hardly any trees or bushes.*

dreary
*She lived in a **dreary** town full of dirty grey buildings.*

gloomy (2) ADJECTIVE

If people are **gloomy**, they are unhappy and not at all hopeful.

dejected
*She felt **dejected** when she didn't win.*

glum
*Angela felt **glum** when the time came to leave her new pet friend.*

sad
*After his gerbil died, John felt **sad**.*

→ down in the dumps

glow VERB

If something **glows**, it shines with a steady dull light.

gleam
*The polished brass knocker **gleamed** in the torchlight.*

glimmer
*It was getting dark when they saw a light **glimmering** in a cottage window.*

shine
*The paintwork on Dad's new car **shone** in the sunlight.*

smoulder
*The remains of the bonfire were still **smouldering** the next day.*

glue

glue NOUN

Glue is a thick sticky liquid used for joining things together.

adhesive
*By the time they finished, their fingers were sticky with **adhesive**.*

cement
*I need some **cement** for my model aircraft.*

gum
*Nicola spread **gum** carefully on the back of her drawing.*

paste
*"We'll use this **paste** to make our collages," said the art teacher.*

go (1) VERB

If you **go** somewhere, you move or travel there.

depart
*Fred saw his sister **depart** in a flurry of bags and cases.*

disappear
*I watched Dad **disappear** downstairs to get my supper.*

leave
*"He'll **leave** as soon as we mention the washing-up," said Auntie.*

travel
*I would like to **travel** round the world when I'm older.*

vanish
*We watched the magician **vanish** in a puff of smoke.*

go (2) VERB

If something such as a watch **goes**, it works properly.

function
*This won't **function** without batteries.*

work
*My watch doesn't **work** because I dropped it in the bath.*

go (3) VERB

If something **goes** with something else, they belong together.

belong
*Where does this screw **belong**?*

fit
*I think that bit of the jigsaw **fits** there.*

go (4) NOUN

A **go** is an attempt to do something.

attempt
*The dung beetle failed to take off on the first **attempt**.*

shot
*"I'd like another **shot** at that. I'm sure I can do it," said Mary.*

stab
*Sue had a **stab** at making a clay pot, but it collapsed in a heap.*

try
*Move the target closer before you have another **try**.*

turn
*"That's not fair!" cried Marta. "It's my **turn** next!"*

good (1) ADJECTIVE

If something like a book or film is **good**, people like it.

brilliant
*The new action film was **brilliant**.*

enjoyable
*We had an **enjoyable** afternoon playing on the swings.*

excellent
*It was an **excellent** game of football but it ended in a draw.*

exciting
*Robert had such an **exciting** ride on the big dipper.*

fabulous
*Our holiday trip to the theme park was really **fabulous**.*

fantastic
*The magician showed the audience some **fantastic** tricks.*

great
*It was such a **great** film, that Lewis wanted to see it again.*

gripping
*It was a **gripping** story. Floella couldn't put the book down.*

thrilling
*Most of the film was boring but it had a **thrilling** ending.*

wonderful
*Thomas sighed happily. "It's been a **wonderful** day. Thank you."*

good (2) ADJECTIVE

Someone who is **good** at something is skilful and successful at it.

bright
*Sam's really **bright** at history. He always comes top.*

clever
*Mum's **clever** with plants. Everything grows for her.*

expert
*You need an **expert** plumber to sort out that tangle of pipes.*

skilful
*The juggler was so **skilful** he could keep several plates in the air at once.*

skilled
*Our doctor is very **skilled**. He knew at once what to do.*

talented
*The music teacher thought Julian was a **talented** violinist.*

good (3) ADJECTIVE

A child or animal that is **good** is well-behaved and obedient.

polite
*Robin was always **polite** when his family had visitors.*

well-behaved
*My dog is **well-behaved**. He never tries to run away.*

good (4) ADJECTIVE

Someone who is **good** is kind and caring and can be trusted.

caring
*My grandma is a gentle, **caring** person.*

helpful
*That lady gave us some **helpful** advice.*

kind
*My knee hurt but the nurse was very **kind**.*

thoughtful
*"Thanks for the cup of tea," said Mum. "It was **thoughtful** of you."*

a b c d e f **Gg** h i j k l m n o p q r s t u v w x y z

grab

grab VERB

If you **grab** something, you take hold of it suddenly and roughly.

clutch
She clutched at her bag before the thief could make off with it.

grasp
The old lady grasped the handrail to stop herself falling down the steps.

seize
Mark seized his jacket and flew out of the door.

snatch
Joel snatched a sandwich before his mum could stop him.

graceful ADJECTIVE

Someone or something that is **graceful** moves in a smooth, pleasant way.

effortless
She turned towards them with an effortless swing of her body.

elegant
The famous actress crossed the stage with elegant movements.

flowing
His pencil quickly covered the page with flowing lines.

smooth
They stood watching the smooth glide of a swan on the river.

supple
Dancers moved around each other with supple ease.

grateful ADJECTIVE

If you are **grateful** for something that someone has done, you want to thank them.

appreciative
Mum likes having my friends to tea because they're so appreciative.

indebted
They felt indebted to the old man for all the help he had given them.

obliged
"I'm obliged to you," said the fairy, as Mary freed her from the cobweb.

thankful
We were thankful to see supper was ready because we were ravenous.

grave ADJECTIVE

Something that is **grave** is important, serious and worrying.

gloomy
We knew the news was bad as soon as we saw his gloomy expression.

serious
"I'm afraid her condition is serious," said the doctor.

solemn
The head teacher made the announcement in solemn tones.

sombre
I noticed the postman looked unusually sombre today.

worrying
There was a worrying lack of medical supplies in the war zone.

great (1) ADJECTIVE

You say something is **great** when it is large in size, number or amount.

colossal
*The Titanic was a **colossal** ship in height and width.*

enormous
*Charles took his **enormous** pet out for a walk.*

gigantic
*The whole thing was a **gigantic** muddle.*

huge
*I think I've made a **huge** mistake.*

immense
*To Jackson's **immense** relief, the puppy was saved.*

mammoth
*The toyshop has got a **mammoth** sale on.*

vast
*They came across a **vast** area where nothing grew.*

great (2) ADJECTIVE

Great also means important.

celebrated
*Picasso painted many **celebrated** pictures.*

famous
*We need someone **famous** to address the crowd.*

grand
*A **grand** staircase curved upwards from the hall.*

important
*Sir Isaac Newton was an **important** scientist and mathematician.*

great (3) ADJECTIVE

Great can mean wonderful.

excellent
*Sirah had an **excellent** time on her beach holiday in Greece.*

fantastic
*"The skateboarding display was **fantastic**," said Jacob.*

terrific
*We gave our teacher a **terrific** send-off when she left to have a baby.*

tremendous
*The film was **tremendous**. It really scared my dad.*

greedy ADJECTIVE

Someone who is **greedy** wants more than they need of something.

gluttonous
*They were horrified by the ogre's **gluttonous** behaviour at dinner.*

grasping
*Scrooge was a **grasping** old man who hoarded his money.*

piggish
*Nobody likes him because of the **piggish** way he gobbles his food.*

selfish
*She's a **selfish** little girl who won't share her toys.*

voracious
*I'm surprised Beth is such a small baby because she has a **voracious** appetite.*

grief NOUN

Someone who feels **grief** is very sad, often because a person or animal they love has died.

distress

When Michel's best friend moved away they both showed signs of **distress**.

heartache

He wasn't prepared for the **heartache** that followed the death of his hamster.

misery

We couldn't find any way of helping Daniel get over his **misery**.

sadness

It was the **sadness** in her eyes that told us what had happened.

sorrow

It was a time of great **sorrow** for the whole family.

grim ADJECTIVE

If someone looks **grim**, they seem worried or angry about something.

bad-tempered

Mr Jones had a **bad-tempered** expression when he handed back our ball.

grave

The head teacher looked **grave** when he told us about the accident.

serious

Tim knew something was wrong when he saw her **serious** face.

severe

His mouth was set in a **severe** line. "What have you been up to?" he asked.

unfriendly

I try not to go in that shop because the man always looks so **unfriendly**.

ground NOUN

The **ground** is the surface of the earth or the floor of a room.

dirt

She dropped her bread jam-side-down on the **dirt**.

earth

It hadn't rained for more than three weeks and the **earth** was parched.

land

The **land** at the back of the house looked perfect for a small garden.

soil

The gardener spent the morning digging the **soil**.

group (1) NOUN

A **group** of things or people is a number of them that are linked together in some way.

crowd

We looked at the **crowd** of people gathered around him.

mob

A **mob** of monkeys attacked the car.

party

At lunchtime a **party** of elderly people arrived in a coach.

group (2) VERB

To **group** things or people means to link them together.

arrange

I **arranged** my books neatly in alphabetical order.

organize

We had to **organize** ourselves into teams.

OTHER GROUPS:
a bunch of grapes
a clutch of eggs
a flock of sheep
a herd of cows
a litter of puppies
a pack of wolves
a pride of lions
a school of dolphins
a shoal of fish
a swarm of bees

a flock of sheep

a pack of wolves

a pride of lions

a school of dolphins

a shoal of fish

grow

grow (1) VERB

To **grow** means to increase in size or amount.

develop
Acorns develop into oak trees.

expand
Our local bookshop is expanding now people are buying more books.

get bigger
When you get bigger, you'll understand.

get taller
Once I get taller I'll be able to reach that high shelf.

increase
The number of people coming to live in the village is increasing.

multiply
The number of rabbits tends to multiply rapidly in spring.

grow (2) VERB

When plants **grow**, they are alive and do well.

flourish
Cacti flourish when you don't water them too much.

germinate
Grass seeds germinate quite quickly.

spring up
Weeds seemed to spring up the minute she turned her back.

sprout
During the spring, leaves begin to sprout everywhere.

grow (3) VERB

To **grow** can mean to change gradually.

become
At night in the desert it becomes much colder.

get
The boys were getting hungry.

turn
The seedlings gradually turned into tall plants with beautiful flowers.

guard VERB

If you **guard** a person or object, you stay near them to keep them safe.

protect
*Nicholas was always ready to **protect** his younger brother.*

shelter
*Tender young plants need **sheltering** from the frost.*

shield
*They wore hats to **shield** them from the harmful rays of the sun.*

watch over
*The dog was left to **watch over** the house while they were out.*

guess VERB

If you **guess** something, you give an answer without knowing if it is right.

believe
*"I **believe** our house is about ten metres high," said Abdullah.*

estimate
*Can you **estimate** how long this cleaning job will take?*

imagine
*"I **imagine** he's missed the train again," said Petra.*

suppose
*Mum said, "I **suppose** you're too tired to watch TV, then?"*

suspect
*I **suspect** he didn't intend to come.*

think
*They **thought** the new music teacher would be older.*

guide (1) VERB

If you **guide** someone, you show them where to go or what to do.

accompany
*We'll need an adult to **accompany** us through the wood.*

direct
*It was a complicated journey and people had to **direct** them at every turn.*

escort
*The teacher promised to **escort** Ben.*

lead
*Lawrence offered to **lead** the others because he'd been there before.*

steer
*Karen discovered it's not all that easy to **steer** a pony.*

usher
*A lady with a torch **ushered** us to our cinema seats.*

guide (2) VERB

If someone or something **guides** you, they affect what you do.

advise
*My sister says the school will **advise** her on a choice of career.*

affect
*The weather will **affect** our plans for a picnic.*

influence
*Matt will be **influenced** by his brother.*

guilty ADJECTIVE

If you feel **guilty**, you are unhappy because you have done something wrong.

ashamed
*Rachel felt **ashamed** about her behaviour.*

sheepish
*The boys looked **sheepish** when their mum saw the mess.*

sorry
*I felt **sorry** about making the baby cry.*

a b c d e f **Gg** h i j k l m n o p q r s t u v w x y z

Hh

habit NOUN

A **habit** is something you do often, sometimes without thinking about it.

custom
*It was his **custom** to take the dog for a walk every night after supper.*

routine
*She cleaned the house every day as a matter of **routine**.*

tradition
*It has become a **tradition** to go to Grandma's for Sunday lunch.*

way
*It is Dad's **way** to polish the car at the weekend.*

hairy ADJECTIVE

Something or someone **hairy** is covered in hair.

bristly
*Dad rubbed his **bristly** chin thoughtfully. "I think I can manage that," he said.*

furry
*A hamster is a small **furry** rodent that sleeps during the day.*

shaggy
*Our dog has got a long **shaggy** coat.*

woolly
*I had a nice **woolly** jacket for my birthday.*

handle (1) VERB

If you **handle** something, you touch or feel it with your hands.

feel
*She liked to **feel** the cool sand as she built sandcastles on the beach.*

finger
*Don't **finger** that pear unless you're going to eat it.*

hold
*He liked picking up spiders, but they were difficult to **hold**.*

stroke
*Lily **stroked** the kitten and made it purr.*

touch
*We **touched** the baby hamsters gently.*

handle (2) VERB

If you agree to **handle** something, you say you will do it.

control
*The teacher asked him to **control** the sale of tickets at the door.*

cope with
*Can you **cope with** the plates while I make the tea?*

deal with
*Sebastian offered to **deal with** the washing-up.*

look after
*Mrs Smith said she would **look after** the flower arrangements.*

manage
*Will you be able to **manage** the rest if I leave now?*

supervise
*I need to **supervise** the face painting.*

hang VERB

If you **hang** something up, you fix it so that it does not touch the ground.

drape
*Trudy **draped** a blanket around her shoulders to keep out the cold.*

fasten
*Spencer **fastened** a large picture above the fireplace.*

fix
*We couldn't decide where to **fix** the mirror in the bathroom.*

suspend
*They **suspended** a lantern from inside the top of the tent.*

happen VERB

If something **happens**, it takes place.

arise
*If anything should **arise** that causes problems, let the teacher know.*

come about
*I don't know how it **came about**, but I found I was in charge.*

crop up
*You never know what can **crop up** at a time like this.*

occur
*It was beginning to get dark when the incident **occurred**.*

take place
*Where exactly are you expecting this party to **take place**?*

happy ADJECTIVE

If you are **happy**, you feel good because most things are the way you want.

bright
*She always has a **bright** smile for everyone she meets.*

cheerful
*It rained all day, but Dad was still bright and **cheerful**.*

contented
*The others moaned, but Jeremiah was quite **contented**.*

delighted
*Mum was **delighted** with her present.*

glad
*I'm **glad** our new teacher is friendly.*

joyful
*The dog gave a **joyful** bark as soon as he saw Tim.*

light-hearted
*The musical we performed was a **light-hearted** affair.*

overjoyed
*Dan was **overjoyed** at the results of his hard work.*

pleased
*Esther was really **pleased** to be going home again.*

thrilled
*Sean was **thrilled** to be chosen to play Peter Pan.*

→ over the moon; walking on air

ANTONYM: **sad**

a b c d e f g **Hh** i j k l m n o p q r s t u v w x y z

hard

hard (1) ADJECTIVE

An object that is **hard** is very firm and stiff.

firm
The mattress felt much too firm.

solid
They stepped cautiously, trying to stand on solid ground.

stiff
His new jeans felt stiff and uncomfortable.

strong
The champion weightlifter had incredibly strong muscles.

hard (2) ADJECTIVE

If something is **hard** to do, it takes a lot of effort.

exhausting
The hike home in the sun was exhausting.

tiring
Luke doesn't like cycling. He says it's too tiring.

tough
It was a tough climb, but we made it.

hard (3) ADJECTIVE

Hard can mean difficult to understand.

complicated
It was a complicated question but I think I got the answer right.

difficult
Some of the problems we have to deal with are really difficult.

harm VERB

To **harm** means to injure someone or damage something.

damage
The use of too many chemicals can damage the environment.

hurt
It won't hurt her to do a bit of work for a change.

ill-treat
The children were taught never to ill-treat an animal.

injure
He beat down the brambles so that they would not injure anybody.

ruin
"Careless washing could ruin this delicate material," said Amanda.

wound
It was obvious the arrow was meant to wound him.

harsh ADJECTIVE

Harsh conditions are severe, difficult and unpleasant.

cruel
Rain and a cruel wind cut through his clothes and froze him to the bone.

hard
Dickens's stories tell how hard life was in Victorian London.

merciless
Few people survive the merciless conditions of this desert.

severe
A severe winter made things difficult for the farmers.

hate VERB

If you **hate** something, you have a strong feeling of dislike for it.

be sick of
*Mum said she **was sick of** doing the washing-up by herself.*

despise
*I **despise** the way he tried to cheat. It was really underhand.*

detest
*"I really **detest** going to football matches,"said Veronica.*

dislike
*Greg **disliked** the way his sister got her way by crying.*

loathe
*"I **loathe** tea," said Mark crossly. "I asked for hot chocolate."*

have (1) VERB

If you **have** something, you own or possess it.

keep
*"Can I **keep** this pen?" asked Tom.*

own
*"Exactly how many books do you **own**?" queried Angus.*

possess
*A good president must **possess** strong leadership skills.*

have (2) VERB

If you **have** something like a good time, you experience it.

experience
*"I **experience** an amazing feeling of excitement," said the skydiver.*

feel
*My sister **felt** great happiness on her wedding day.*

healthy (1) ADJECTIVE

Someone who is **healthy** is well and is not suffering from any illness.

fit
*Grandma keeps **fit** by walking every day.*

in good shape INFORMAL
*Ken has to stay **in good shape** for his job.*

sound
*The doctor said her heart was **sound**.*

strong
*Our football coach is very **strong**.*

well
*I can't go to camp unless I'm **well**.*

ANTONYM: ill

healthy (2) ADJECTIVE

Something that is **healthy** is good for you.

bracing
*What you need is a **bracing** walk.*

good for you
*Greens are **good for you**, so eat them up.*

nourishing
*Our cat still looks skinny though it eats lots of **nourishing** food.*

wholesome
*Mum's cakes are too **wholesome** for me.*

ANTONYM: unhealthy

heap NOUN

A **heap** is a lot of things piled up, usually rather untidily.

mass
*His bed was covered with a **mass** of discarded clothes.*

mound
*Mum sighed at the **mound** of ironing waiting to be done.*

pile
*There was a huge **pile** of books to read.*

stack
*Next to the sink was a **stack** of dirty plates.*

help VERB

If you **help** someone, you make things better or easier for them.

assist

The children **assisted** each other with their history project.

give a hand

"Come on," she shouted. "**Give** me **a hand**, can't you?"

improve

If you work a bit harder, it will **improve** your chances.

lend a hand

My brother couldn't manage on his own, so I **lent a hand**.

save

The baby nearly fell over, but I **saved** him.

helpful ADJECTIVE

Someone **helpful** is ready to give assistance or advice.

caring

We've got a **caring** neighbour who feeds the cat when we're away.

friendly

The teachers are always **friendly** if you need anything.

kind

The nurse was very **kind** when I fell and hurt my wrist.

thoughtful

"How **thoughtful** of you," said the king. "I've always wanted one of those!"

willing

Douglas was easily the most **willing** boy in the class.

hesitate VERB

If you **hesitate**, you pause while you are doing something, or before you do it.

delay

The head teacher decided not to **delay**, but to go straight on with his talk.

dither

Rupert **dithered**, trying to think of the right words.

pause

She **paused** and then said, "This applies to all of you."

wait

He **waited** for a moment but nobody offered to help, so he did it himself.

hide (1) VERB

If you **hide** somewhere, you go where you cannot be seen.

lie low

He decided to **lie low** until all the fuss was over.

take cover

They **took cover** in an old shed until the danger was past.

hide (2) VERB

If you **hide** something, you cover it or put it in a place where it can't be seen.

conceal

She **concealed** the scar on her throat with a scarf.

cover

Mum **covered** the hole in the carpet with a rug.

hit (1) VERB

If you **hit** something, you touch it quickly and hard.

beat
He beat the drum as hard as he could.

clout
A falling branch clouted me on my right shoulder.

knock
Laura accidentally knocked her head on the doorframe.

punch
She tried to punch Ben on the nose, but he ducked.

slap
Roger's the jolly sort of person who slaps you on the back.

smack
A twig sprang back and smacked Sam in the face.

strike
Nista struck the ball and it flew over to the boundary.

stub
My brother cried when he stubbed his toe on the step.

thump
"I won't have it!" he shouted, and thumped the table.

whack
Andrew whacked the ball hard back over the net.

hit (2) VERB

If you **hit** something, you collide with it.

bang
I banged my head on the shelf.

bump
Terry fell down and bumped his knee.

bump into
Ruben couldn't stop in time and bumped into the fence.

crash into
Freddie skidded on the ice and then crashed into a dustbin.

run into
Dad ran into the back of another car.

smash into
A boat smashed into the harbour wall.

hoarse ADJECTIVE

A **hoarse** voice sounds rough.

croaky
Nina's cold left her too croaky to talk for long.

gruff
"Dad sounds gruff," said Mel, "but he's really nice."

husky
"That husky voice is just right!" cried the drama teacher.

rasping
"My throat's awfully sore," said the dragon in rasping tones.

hold

hold (1) VERB

When you **hold** something, you keep it in your hand or arms.

carry
*Can you **carry** this bag for me, please?*

clasp
*He **clasped** the kitten to him and buried his face in its fur.*

clutch
*Emily **clutched** her mother's hand in sudden panic.*

cradle
*Stuart **cradled** the new baby carefully in his arms.*

embrace
*Dad ran along the platform and **embraced** us both.*

grip
*Gus **gripped** his little brother's hand as they crossed the road.*

hug
*Ellie **hugged** her teddy bear and sang it a song.*

hold (2) VERB

If something **holds** a particular amount of something, it can contain that amount.

accommodate
*The caravan will **accommodate** two adults and four children.*

carry
*Our new car **carries** six people in comfort.*

contain
*That barrel **contains** enough water for hundreds of plants.*

take
*The picnic basket will **take** food for ten.*

hole NOUN

A **hole** is an opening or space in something.

burrow
*A rabbit stuck its head out of a **burrow** just as a fox was passing.*

cave
*There was a large **cave** in the hillside and they couldn't resist a look.*

crack
*Two men were fishing through a **crack** in the ice.*

crater
*Huge **craters** can be seen on the surface of the planet.*

gap
*They peered through a **gap** in the fence and saw a pile of rubbish.*

leak
*Mind the water on the floor. The pipe's got a **leak**.*

pit
*The pirates worked all afternoon, digging a **pit** to hide their treasure.*

pothole
*Marshall hit a **pothole** in the road and came off his bike.*

tear
*Mum groaned when she saw the **tear** in my jeans.*

tunnel
*The rabbit dug a **tunnel** under the fence and escaped.*

honest ADJECTIVE

Someone who is **honest** tells the truth and can be trusted.

law-abiding
*Mr Thomson is very **law-abiding**. He always parks carefully.*

sincere
*My sister said she wanted my **sincere** opinion of her new hairstyle.*

trustworthy
*Jude's **trustworthy**, so we'll ask her to collect the money.*

truthful
*The teacher said she only wanted a **truthful** report.*

hopeless (1) ADJECTIVE

You say a situation is **hopeless** when it is very bad and you do not think it will get better.

desperate
*The tide was coming in and their situation was **desperate**.*

futile
*He decided his efforts were **futile**.*

impossible
*Kelly said the whole project was **impossible** and they should give up.*

pointless
*"This is a **pointless** exercise," said Robin finally.*

useless
*"Shouting is **useless**," sneered the witch. "Nobody can hear you."*

vain
*They struggled hard in a **vain** attempt to shift the rock.*

hopeless (2) ADJECTIVE

If somebody is **hopeless** at doing something, they cannot do it well.

incompetent
*The plumber was **incompetent** and all the pipes leaked.*

no good
*Grandad's **no good** at dancing, but he doesn't let that stop him.*

poor
*Uncle Eddie is so **poor** at DIY all his shelves fall down.*

useless
*She might be **useless** as a cricketer, but she's a brilliant friend.*

horrible ADJECTIVE

Someone or something that is **horrible** is awful or unpleasant.

awful
*I've got an **awful** headache.*

horrid
*He was a **horrid** little man with foul-smelling breath.*

mean
*She played a really **mean** trick on him.*

nasty
*The crocodile bared its sharp teeth in a **nasty** smile.*

unpleasant
*The weather was too **unpleasant** for us to play outside.*

a b c d e f g **Hh** i j k l m n o p q r s t u v w x y z

hot

hot (1) ADJECTIVE
Something or someone that is **hot** has a high temperature.

baking
It was **baking** outdoors so we sat in the shade under a tree.

blazing
The camels trudged across the desert under the **blazing** sun.

boiling
Grandpa hates the cold, so it's always **boiling** in his house.

burning
The nurse laid a cool hand on Christopher's **burning** forehead.

feverish
He felt **feverish** and his throat was sore, so his mum sent for the doctor.

scalding
The water in the bath was **scalding**, so she added cold.

ANTONYM: cold

hot (2) ADJECTIVE
You say food is **hot** if it has a strong spicy taste.

peppery
The meal was a bit too **peppery** for me.

spicy
Dad likes his curries really **spicy**.

ANTONYM: mild

hungry ADJECTIVE
When you are **hungry**, you want to eat.

famished
"Fee, fi, fo, fum!" roared the huge ogre. "I'm **famished**."

peckish
"I expect you're **peckish**," she said, and piled the plate high.

ravenous
We were **ravenous** after our swim.

starving
Starving birds pecked at the seeds we put out in the garden.

hurry VERB
If you **hurry** somewhere, you go there as quickly as you can.

dash
Patch **dashed** off towards home.

fly
Collin heard his dad coming and **flew** to meet him.

get a move on
If we don't **get a move on** we'll be late for the party.

run
She **ran** all the way to school and arrived just before the bell rang.

rush
Adam **rushes** everywhere.

scurry
A mouse **scurried** across the floor and out of the back door.

hurt (1) VERB

If part of your body **hurts**, you feel pain.

ache
*My tooth has been **aching** all day.*

smart
*Smoke from the bonfire blew in his face and made his eyes **smart**.*

sting
*Tamzin's cut **stung** when she put cream on it.*

tingle
*His leg **tingled** where he'd brushed against the nettles.*

throb
*The music was so loud that his head began to **throb**.*

hurt (2) VERB

If you have been **hurt**, you have been injured.

damage
*The doctor told them Damien's eye was slightly **damaged**.*

harm
*Luckily I wasn't **harmed** when glass in the window broke.*

injure
*A lot of people were **injured** in the motorway accident.*

maim
*If the branch had fallen on him, he could have been **maimed** or killed.*

wound
*I **wounded** my knee when I fell off the bike.*

hurt (3) VERB

To **hurt** someone can mean to upset them.

distress
*You must be careful not to **distress** the new hamster.*

sadden
*It **saddened** Petra to think of her friend moving away.*

torment
*You'd better stop **tormenting** that cat or it will scratch you.*

upset
*Don't say anything to Grandma. It will only **upset** her.*

hurt (4) ADJECTIVE

If you feel **hurt**, you are upset or offended.

distress
*She was **distressed***

grieved
*Peter was **grieved** by his friend's refusal to talk to him.*

insulted
*Atlas was **insulted** when someone said he was feeble.*

offended
*The old lady was **offended** when I tried to help her cross the road.*

upset
*Stefan was **upset** to see the state of his new mountain bike.*

Ii

idea NOUN

If you have an **idea**, you suddenly think of a way of doing something.

brainwave
*Harriet had a sudden **brainwave** and solved the problem.*

plan
*I've thought of a **plan** to get some money.*

scheme
*That's just another of his mad **schemes**.*

suggestion
*The head teacher didn't think much of the **suggestion**.*

ill ADJECTIVE

Someone who is **ill** has something wrong with their health.

ailing
*The king was **ailing**, so the princess played some music to cheer him up.*

queasy
*I always feel **queasy** on boats.*

sick
*Fabio's mum said he was too **sick** to go to school.*

unwell
*The clown came on with a giant ice pack on his head and said he was **unwell**.*

illness NOUN

An **illness** is something like a cold or measles that people can suffer from.

ailment
*His sister's always complaining of some **ailment** or other.*

bug
*Lizzie was off school with a stomach **bug** last week.*

disease
*Polluted water can cause terrible **diseases**.*

imaginary ADJECTIVE

Something that is **imaginary** is not real. It is only in your mind.

dreamlike
*The whole of the afternoon had a **dreamlike** quality.*

fanciful
*Becky is full of **fanciful** tales about having a pet dragon.*

fictitious
*Peter Pan is a **fictitious** character.*

invented
*Nearly all of her so-called adventures are **invented**.*

made-up
*"I don't believe you," said Jim. "I think that is a **made-up** story."*

unreal
*It all felt **unreal**, as if he were in a film.*

important (1) ADJECTIVE

If someone says something is **important**, they mean it matters a lot.

basic
Basic equipment for camping includes a good tent.

big
*The next **big** event is the school play.*

essential
*Water is **essential** for all living things.*

main
*"The **main** thing is that you all enjoy yourselves," said the dance teacher.*

major
*Exercise is a **major** part of staying healthy.*

necessary
*Fitness and common sense are **necessary** qualities for a good rock climber.*

serious
*At the last minute they discovered a **serious** flaw in their plan.*

special
*Mum and Dad are celebrating another **special** anniversary.*

important (2) ADJECTIVE

Someone who is **important** has a lot of power in a particular group.

famous
*We're going to meet a **famous** film star.*

high-ranking
*His dad's a **high-ranking** police officer.*

leading
*Esmeralda had a **leading** part in the school play.*

powerful
*The President of the United States is in a **powerful** position.*

impressive ADJECTIVE

If something is **impressive**, people admire it, usually because it is large or important.

awe-inspiring
*Edmund gazed up at the mountain. It was **awe-inspiring**.*

grand
*They came upon a huge house with a **grand** garden.*

great
*I stared at the **great** stone statue in the hotel courtyard.*

magnificent
*The trees were **magnificent**. They were the tallest he'd ever seen.*

increase VERB

If something **increases**, it becomes greater.

expand
*As he became older his waistline **expanded** alarmingly.*

extend
*The school is hoping to **extend** the size of the playing fields.*

grow
*The number of students at the school is expected to **grow** next year.*

multiply
*These germs can spread easily and **multiply** rapidly.*

rise
*The teacher was pleased that the number of children using the library had **risen**.*

ANTONYM: **decrease**

informal

informal ADJECTIVE

Informal means relaxed and casual.

casual
On Friday we can wear **casual** clothes to school.

easy
Our doctor has a very **easy** manner.

friendly
It was just a **friendly** match.

natural
He wasn't at all pompous and just chatted in a **natural** way.

relaxed
It was a very **relaxed** interview.

information NOUN

If someone gives you **information** about something, they tell you about it.

facts
The police said they had several leads in the case, but needed more **facts**.

material
You'll find plenty of **material** on this subject in the library.

news
The soldier's friends and family were anxiously awaiting **news**.

notice
We'll get plenty of **notice** nearer the time.

word
The head teacher said he'd received **word** that a famous author was coming.

insect NOUN

An **insect** is a small animal with six legs. It usually has wings.

SOME INSECTS:
ant
bee
beetle
butterfly
dragonfly
fly
grasshopper
ladybird
wasp

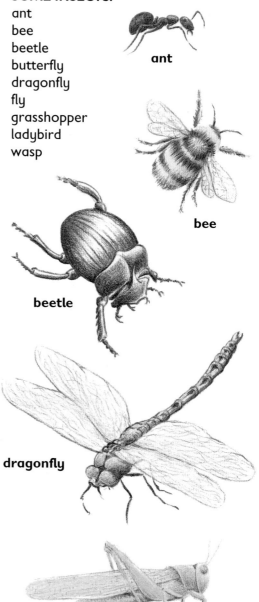

ant

bee

beetle

dragonfly

grasshopper

ladybird

interesting ADJECTIVE

If something is **interesting**, it attracts or holds your attention.

amazing

"That is an **amazing** firework display," said Toni.

amusing

His uncle knows lots of **amusing** stories about animals.

entertaining

The girls watched an **entertaining** programme on the television.

exciting

Andy leads an **exciting** life as an explorer.

fascinating

Grandma said she found my polar bear story **fascinating**.

gripping

The plot was so **gripping** George couldn't put the book down.

intriguing

The police found the mystery **intriguing**.

unusual

The dog dug up an **unusual** object.

invent VERB

If someone **invents** something such as a machine, they are the first person to think of it.

come up with

His mum asked him to **come up with** a name for her shop.

create

I'd like to **create** a robot to do my homework and tidy my room.

design

They were asked to **design** a new way of packing eggs.

devise

Billy tried to **devise** a way of opening the door without getting up.

plan

We **planned** a different layout for the new train set.

think up

It's not easy to **think up** something completely new.

invisible ADJECTIVE

If something is **invisible**, it cannot be seen.

concealed

The conjuror made sure everything was **concealed** ready for the tricks.

disguised

Chameleons can become **disguised** when they change colour.

hidden

A leopard was **hidden** in the dappled shade of the trees.

microscopic

Out there is a whole world of things that are **microscopic**.

ANTONYM: **visible**

Jj

jagged ADJECTIVE

Something **jagged** has an uneven edge with sharp points on it.

broken
*The wall was topped with **broken** glass.*

rough
*Steven tore his sleeve on the **rough** edge of a rock.*

uneven
*She trimmed the photo rapidly with careless, **uneven** cuts.*

jam VERB

If you **jam** something in somewhere, you push it there roughly.

cram
*In a fury, the witch **crammed** her hat on her head and strode out of the door.*

pack
*Aziz **packed** more and more clothes into the case until it was bursting.*

squeeze
*We couldn't see how they were going to **squeeze** us all in.*

jealous ADJECTIVE

Someone who is **jealous** feels upset because someone else has what they want.

envious
*Lizzie was always **envious** of her big sister's new clothes.*

resentful
*Charles was **resentful** of all the attention people paid his baby brother.*

upset
*Sandra will be **upset** if she doesn't get a present too.*

jet NOUN

A **jet** is a stream of liquid or gas forced out under pressure.

fountain
*The firework exploded in a **fountain** of coloured lights.*

gush
*They had to leap back to avoid the sudden **gush** from the tap.*

spray
*Dad sent a **spray** of water over the car to clean it.*

spurt
*There was a small **spurt** of blood when Debbie cut her finger.*

squirt
*A **squirt** of ink from the fountain pen went across his homework.*

jewel NOUN

A **jewel** is a precious stone, such as a diamond or a ruby, used to make things like rings and necklaces.

gem
*Her ring had a single **gem** set in silver.*

gemstone
*The duchess wore a tiara sparkling with rare **gemstones**.*

ornament
*King Ralph wore several valuable **ornaments** around his neck.*

precious stone
*Her earrings twinkled with **precious stones**.*

rock
*The singer wore **rocks** the size of marbles on his fingers.*

stone
*"What a beautiful **stone**," gushed Sandra. "Was it expensive?"*

job (1) NOUN

A **job** is the work that someone does to earn money.

employment
*Dad says the new building will bring plenty of **employment**.*

occupation
*Firefighting is a dangerous **occupation**.*

work
*"What **work** does your mum do?" asked Sebastian casually.*

job (2) NOUN

A **job** can be anything that has to be done.

chore
*I have to do **chores** like making my bed before I go to school.*

errand
*Ron had a few **errands** to do before he met his friends.*

task
*Our first **task** was to make a timetable.*

SOME JOBS PEOPLE DO:

actor
architect
artist
builder
chemist
cook
dentist
designer
doctor

electrician
engineer
farmer
firefighter
lawyer
librarian
musician
nurse

optician
plumber
police officer
postman/woman
scientist
teacher
vet
writer

musician

firefighter

artist

vet

farmer

join

a
b
c
d
e
f
g
h
i
Jj
k
l
m
n
o
p
q
r
s
t
u
v
w
x
y
z

join (1) VERB

If you **join** a club or organization, you become a member of it.

become a member of
I've **become a member of** the local library.

enlist in
My brother is planning to **enlist in** the army when he finishes school.

enrol in
Jessie wanted to **enrol in** the dancing class.

join (2) VERB

To **join** can mean to fasten two things together.

attach
He **attached** the pages with a clip.

connect
Dad tried to **connect** two pipes, but they came unstuck.

fix
They had to **fix** the sides of the box with adhesive tape.

stick
Abdul **stuck** the wings on with glue.

tie
Clare **tied** the ends of the ribbon in a bow.

join (3) VERB

When things **join**, they come together.

border on
Philomena's garden **borders on** the most beautiful countryside.

combine
This clever play manages to **combine** terror with comedy.

come together
The two footpaths **came together** in a sunlit clearing.

meet
We arranged to **meet** the others at the railway station.

reach
When they **reached** the main road they found it heavy with traffic.

journey NOUN

If you go on a **journey**, you travel from one place to another.

drive
Dad took us on a **drive** to the seaside.

excursion
The **excursion** was by coach.

expedition
John and Patrick planned an **expedition** to the island.

flight
It is a very long **flight** from London to Sydney.

hike
The **hike** took them deep into the snow-covered mountains.

ride
Lee enjoyed her **ride** to Gran's house.

tour
My brother wants to go on a **tour** to see all the Welsh castles.

trek
They found themselves on an exhausting **trek** through the forest.

trip
The **trip** should have been fun, but it turned out to be rather boring.

voyage
It was a long **voyage**, and Jeremy soon became seasick.

walk
We were looking forward to our five-mile **walk** in the countryside.

judge VERB

If you **judge** someone or something, you form an opinion about them.

appreciate
*You have to know something about art to **appreciate** these paintings.*

assess
*The teacher asked us to **assess** each other's science project.*

consider
*Everyone in the village **considers** Dad's cooking to be fantastic.*

decide
*At the dog show they **decided** Fifi the French poodle should win top prize.*

evaluate
*Three teachers sat on the platform **evaluating** the dancers' performances.*

rate
*The review **rated** Holly's violin playing as exceptional for her age.*

rule
*Finally, the head teacher **ruled** that Chris was the winner.*

sized up
*Mum **sized up** the situation very quickly and sent us both to bed.*

juice NOUN

Juice is the liquid that comes from fruit such as oranges when you squeeze them.

fluid
*He cut the orange in half and **fluid** ran onto the table.*

liquid
*As she squeezed the fruit, drops of **liquid** fell into the cake mixture.*

jump VERB

When you **jump**, you spring off the ground using your leg muscles.

bounce
*Gareth **bounced** up and hit the ball in the air.*

bound
*The kangaroo **bounded** across the ground at great speed.*

hop
*A rabbit **hopped** away in front of them.*

leap
*Jamil watched squirrels **leaping** through the trees.*

pounce
*Our cat likes to **pounce** on mice, but she usually misses.*

skip
*Julia **skipped** up and down when her team scored a goal.*

spring
*He **sprang** up at once and offered to help.*

vault
*Jessie **vaulted** over the gate as the dog raced towards her.*

Kk

keen ADJECTIVE

Someone who is **keen** to do something wants to do it very much.

anxious

Ellie was **anxious** to show how well she could cope.

avid

He was an **avid** supporter of the local football team.

eager

The whole class was **eager** to go on the outing to the zoo.

enthusiastic

Terry only wants people in his team who are **enthusiastic**.

keep (1) VERB

If you **keep** something, you store it.

put

Mum **puts** the house keys in a special box so they don't get lost.

store

Mr Jones **stores** apples in his shed.

stow

I **stow** my toys in the cupboard.

keep (2) VERB

If you **keep** something, you have it and look after it.

care for

The wildlife centre **cares for** otters here.

look after

That lady **looks after** cats that need a good home.

run

His dad **runs** a small sweetshop not far from here.

keep (3) VERB

If you **keep** doing something, you do it over and over again.

carry on

The teacher told him to stop, but he **carried on** doing it.

go on

Aunt Rudy says she'll **go on** working here until she retires.

kill VERB

To **kill** someone or something means to make them die.

assassinate

Powerful people, such as presidents, are sometimes **assassinated**.

destroy

The dog had to be **destroyed** because it was so vicious.

execute

King Charles I was **executed**.

exterminate

Dad has been trying to **exterminate** the slugs in our garden.

murder

To **murder** someone is a terrible crime.

put to sleep

Jade was upset when her cat was so ill it had to be **put to sleep**.

slaughter

All animals affected by the disease had to be **slaughtered**.

slay

The knight set out at once to **slay** the terrifying dragon.

kind (1) ADJECTIVE

Someone who is **kind** behaves in a gentle, caring way.

friendly
*That old lady's quite **friendly**. She always throws our ball back.*

gentle
*I like my dentist. He is very **gentle**.*

helpful
*The librarian's **helpful** when you can't find a book.*

thoughtful
*"It was **thoughtful** of you to bring flowers," she said.*

understanding
*Our teacher's very **understanding** if you don't feel well.*

kind (2) NOUN

If you talk about a **kind** of object, you mean a sort of object.

brand
*What **brand** of cornflakes do you have?*

sort
*John has got all **sorts** of games.*

type
*"I really like this **type** of food," said Uncle Henry.*

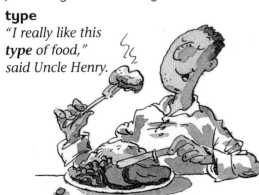

know (1) VERB

If you **know** a fact, you have it in your mind and don't need to learn it.

be certain of
*"I **am certain of** one thing," said Mum. "You're going to bed now."*

be sure of
*David **was sure of** the answer.*

realize
*They suddenly **realized** that they had been tricked.*

see
*You must **see** that your plan won't work.*

understand
*At last he **understood** exactly what the teacher meant.*

know (2) VERB

If you **know** somebody, you have met them before.

identify
*James **identified** the man by his strange, curly moustache.*

recognize
*I would **recognize** him anywhere.*

knowledge NOUN

Knowledge is the information and understanding that you have.

education
Education has helped him get the job he really wanted.

facts
*Don't make up your mind about this until you have enough **facts**.*

information
*Police say they now have all the **information** they need to solve the case.*

learning
*The professor was a man of great **learning** who could talk about anything.*

wisdom
*People who are thoughtful usually gain **wisdom** as they grow older.*

a
b
c
d
e
f
g
h
i
j
Kk
l
m
n
o
p
q
r
s
t
u
v
w
x
y
z

a b c d e f g h i j k **Ll** m n o p q r s t u v w x y z

Ll

land (1) NOUN

Land is the part of the world that is solid, dry ground.

earth
The **earth** was too dry and farmers were desperate for rain.

ground
After the rain, the **ground** was quickly covered with bright green shoots.

soil
He dug lots of compost into the **soil** to help the plants grow.

land (2) NOUN

A **land** is a region or country.

country
"Mexico is a very large **country** in Central America," said the teacher.

nation
Leaders of friendly **nations** meet to discuss important things.

region
Different **regions** of the world have their own climates.

territory
Wars are sometimes fought about the boundaries of **territory**.

land (3) VERB

When a bird or aircraft **lands**, it comes down on to land or water.

alight
A blackbird **alighted** on a branch above their heads.

arrive
The plane was due to **arrive** in Paris in the late afternoon.

come down
They **came down** with hardly a bump, and the journey was over.

come to rest
Wild geese skimmed above the lake and **came to rest** close to the hide.

touch down
"We shall be **touching down** in a few minutes," said the pilot as the jumbo jet began its descent.

last (1) ADJECTIVE

If something happens **last**, it happens after everything else.

closing
The **closing** bars of the music sounded loud and triumphant.

concluding
I almost forgot to read out the **concluding** paragraph of my talk.

final
Charlotte has had a **final** warning about her homework and she is determined to do better next time.

ANTONYM: **first**

last (2) VERB

If something **lasts**, it continues to exist or happen.

carry on
*His speech seemed to **carry on** forever.*

continue
*They were hoping Auntie Anne's good mood would **continue**.*

remain
*The castle has **remained** in reasonable condition for centuries.*

survive
*We needed the car to **survive** at least until the holiday was over.*

laugh VERB

When you **laugh**, you make a sound that shows you think something is funny.

cackle
*"That's really funny," **cackled** the witch.*

giggle
*The two children **giggled** at each other.*

snigger
*The others **sniggered** when they saw my new jumper.*

➔ fall about laughing; laugh your head off; roar with laughter; split your sides

law NOUN

A **law** is a rule that is made by the government.

code
*Drivers are expected to follow strict **codes** of behaviour on the road.*

regulation
*There are **regulations** to control the hours pilots spend flying.*

rule
*An important **rule** is that children go to school regularly.*

lay VERB

If you **lay** something somewhere, you put it there carefully.

place
*They collected the papers and **placed** them on her desk.*

put
*"Just **put** it down anywhere on the table," she said.*

set down
*He **set down** the book in front of her.*

spread
*Dad **spread** a rug on the damp grass.*

layer NOUN

A **layer** is a single thickness of something that lies on top of or underneath something else.

blanket
*A **blanket** of fog hid the landscape.*

coat
*The decorator said the door needed another **coat** of paint.*

coating
*Mum added a thick **coating** of icing sugar to the cake.*

film
*Nothing had disturbed the **film** of dust on the mantelpiece.*

sheet
*The pond was covered with a **sheet** of ice.*

a
b
c
d
e
f
g
h
i
j
k
Ll
m
n
o
p
q
r
s
t
u
v
w
x
y
z

leak

leak NOUN
A **leak** is a hole that lets gas or liquid escape.

chink
*Gas was escaping through a small **chink**.*

crack
*The roots of a tree had caused a **crack** in the waste pipe.*

hole
*Water seeped through several small **holes** in the swimming pool.*

puncture
*She watched the tyre go flat as air hissed from the **puncture**.*

leave VERB
When you **leave** a person or place, you go away from them.

abandon
*One of the sheep **abandoned** its lamb.*

desert
*Our cat would never **desert** her kittens.*

go
*Let's **go** as soon as the play is over.*

resign
*Mum's going to **resign** her position.*

set off
*They **set off** in a frantic rush.*

level ADJECTIVE
A surface that is **level** is smooth, flat and parallel to the ground.

even
*Nothing was allowed to spoil the **even** appearance of the lawn.*

flat
*Shannon needed somewhere **flat** to leave her artwork.*

horizontal
*Every **horizontal** surface held books and piles of papers.*

smooth
*At last the wood was **smooth** and ready to make into a table.*

lie (1) VERB
To **lie** somewhere means to rest there horizontally.

lounge
*My brother just **lounges** about all day.*

recline
*Auntie Hilary **reclined** in a deckchair with a book on her lap.*

rest
*Sebastian wanted to **rest** on the bench after the game of tennis.*

sprawl
*Alexander **sprawled** in the chair with his eyes closed.*

stretch out
*The dog **stretched out** on the floor and went to sleep.*

lie (2) VERB
To **lie** means to say something that is not true.

bluff
*Don't worry about it. He's **bluffing**.*

fib
*She often **fibs** to get out of trouble.*

light (1) ADJECTIVE
A place that is **light** is bright because of the sun or the use of lamps.

airy
*She showed them into a large, **airy** room.*

bright
*It was much **brighter** outside.*

well-lit
*Sue's room was quite small but **well-lit**.*

light (2) ADJECTIVE

A **light** object does not weigh much.

delicate
*Chelsea wore a **delicate**, long-sleeved dress to the party.*

flimsy
*The fairy's wings were **flimsy** and see-through.*

light (3) VERB

To **light** a fire means to make it start burning.

catch fire
*The wood was damp and wouldn't **catch fire** immediately.*

ignite
*Dad **ignited** the rocket and stood well back with the rest of us.*

light (4) ADJECTIVE

A **light** colour is pale.

fair
*Rhiannon's **fair** skin burned very easily in the sun.*

pale
*The sky was a **pale** blue.*

pastel
*My shirt was a **pastel** yellow colour.*

like VERB

If you **like** someone or something, you find them pleasant.

adore
*Sophie **adores** the new puppies.*

enjoy
*What sorts of films do you **enjoy**?*

love
*Our parrot **loves** ginger biscuits.*

→ be crazy about; be mad about

little ADJECTIVE

Someone or something that is **little** is small in size.

brief
*"That skirt is too **brief** to wear outside," said Mum.*

narrow
*A **narrow** path led down through the trees to the river.*

small
*He gave her a **small** bite of his chocolate and nut bar.*

tiny
*The baby wore a **tiny** bracelet on her wrist.*

young
*My brother's only **young**. That's why he doesn't understand.*

lively ADJECTIVE

Someone who is **lively** is cheerful and full of energy.

active
*The baby's always **active** when he's just had a sleep.*

chirpy
*Her grandmother sounded **chirpy** after her visit to the theatre.*

energetic
*Ed felt really **energetic** during the first football game of the season.*

frisky
*Rover grew **frisky** as soon as he saw the ducks on the lake.*

perky
*"He looks much **perkier** today," said the doctor. "Back to school tomorrow!"*

a b c d e f g h i j k **Ll** m n o p q r s t u v w x y z

lonely

lonely (1) ADJECTIVE

Someone who is **lonely** is unhappy because they are on their own, or do not have any friends.

alone
*You can sometimes feel **alone**, even when you are in a crowd.*

forlorn
*Francesco was **forlorn** when his big brother left home.*

friendless
*At first he felt **friendless** at his new school.*

lonesome
*Fluffy is **lonesome** without her kittens.*

unhappy
*The dog seems **unhappy** now Kim's at school all day.*

lonely (2) ADJECTIVE

A **lonely** place is away from towns and is not visited by many people.

isolated
*They stayed in an **isolated** cottage on the edge of a lake.*

remote
*The farmer's sheep grazed quietly on a **remote** hillside.*

secluded
*They found a **secluded** spot far away from the road.*

solitary
*Grandpa grew up in a **solitary** farm with no running water.*

uninhabited
*Through the telescope they saw a small, **uninhabited** island.*

→ off the beaten track; out-of-the-way

look (1) VERB

If you **look** in a particular direction, you turn your eyes that way.

gaze
*She **gazed** at the beautiful countryside around her.*

glance
*Anoop **glanced** across at her, then smiled and waved.*

peep
*Peter **peeped** in through the window.*

peer
*Grandma **peered** at the badge on my denim jacket.*

stare
*Alice **stared** at the White Rabbit as he turned away.*

watch
*From the cliff top they **watched** as men unloaded a small boat.*

look (2) VERB

How someone **looks** is how they appear or seem to be.

appear
*When William arrived at school, he **appeared** anxious.*

seem
*Dad **seemed** pleased about something, but he wouldn't tell us what.*

seem to be
*The baby **seems to be** happier when I'm there to play with her.*

a b c d e f g h i j k **Ll** m n o p q r s t u v w x y z

lump

loud ADJECTIVE
A **loud** sound is one that makes a lot of noise.

deafening
*There was a **deafening** bang as the firework went off.*

harsh
*The raven's cries were **harsh** and unpleasant to listen to.*

noisy
*Mum complained that we were all being too **noisy**.*

piercing
*Rosie gave a **piercing** shriek when she saw the spider.*

shrill
*The old lady's voice was **shrill** with anger.*

thunderous
*One of the lions gave a **thunderous** roar.*

→ ear-piercing; ear-splitting

ANTONYM: quiet

love (1) VERB
If you **love** someone, you have strong feelings of affection for them.

adore
*My brother **adores** his new girlfriend.*

be fond of
*Christopher Robin **was fond of** Pooh Bear.*

worship
*Georgina really **worships** her dad.*

ANTONYM: hate

love (2) VERB
If you **love** something, you like it very much.

enjoy
*Thomas **enjoys** reading.*

like
*I **like** any kind of pasta.*

lump (1) NOUN
A **lump** is a piece of something solid.

ball
*She took a **ball** of modelling clay and began to work.*

cake
*The new **cake** of soap smelled of roses.*

chunk
*One of the ducks gobbled a **chunk** of stale bread.*

piece
*A mysterious **piece** of rock suddenly appeared on the path.*

wedge
*Darcy helped himself to a generous **wedge** of cheese.*

lump (2) NOUN
A **lump** can be a bump on the surface of something.

bulge
*He tried to pretend he wasn't eating anything, but there was a suspicious **bulge** in his cheek.*

bump
*The road was terrible but they tried to avoid the worst of the **bumps**.*

swelling
*Thomas had a **swelling** over one eye after the fight.*

a
b
c
d
e
f
g
h
i
j
k
l
Mm
n
o
p
q
r
s
t
u
v
w
x
y
z

Mm

magic NOUN

In stories, **magic** is the thing that makes impossible things happen.

SOME KINDS OF MAGIC:

conjuring
enchantment
hocus-pocus
illusion

spells
trickery
witchcraft
wizardry

magical ADJECTIVE

Something that is **magical** is wonderful and exciting.

fascinating
*The magician wore a cloak covered in **fascinating** designs.*

marvellous
*We had a **marvellous** tree completely covered in decorations.*

spellbinding
*The lights in the city were **spellbinding**.*

main ADJECTIVE

The **main** part of something is the most important part.

basic
*Remember, the **basic** requirement for a singer is talent.*

chief
*He outlined the **chief** things he wanted to cover during the lesson.*

essential
*"Grass and hay are the **essential** foods for our cows," said the farmer.*

leading
*The **leading** actress in the film is famous in Japan.*

major
*The **major** reason for Alison's success is hard work.*

make (1) VERB

If you **make** something new, you use your skill to shape it or put it together.

assemble
*My model aircraft was quite difficult to **assemble**.*

build
*The third little pig **built** his house of bricks.*

form
*Oliver **formed** a cat out of clay.*

invent
*My dad's trying to **invent** a new kind of mini camera.*

put together
*They **put together** all the scenery for the train set.*

make (2) VERB

If you **make** someone do something, you force them to do it.

force
*She didn't want to hand over her money but the highwayman **forced** her.*

order
*The soldiers were **ordered** to retreat.*

mammal NOUN

A **mammal** is a warm-blooded animal. Female mammals give birth to live babies. They feed their babies with milk from their own bodies.

FARM MAMMALS:
cow
goat
horse
pig
sheep

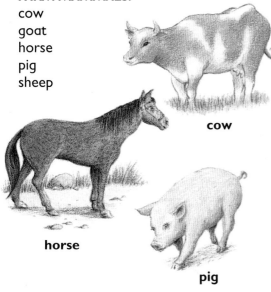

cow

horse

pig

MAMMALS THAT LIVE IN OR NEAR WATER:
dolphin
hippopotamus
otter
seal
walrus
whale

hippopotamus

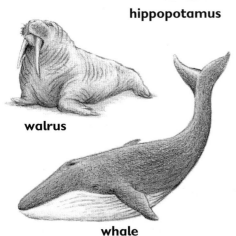

walrus

whale

PET MAMMALS:
cat
dog
gerbil
guinea pig
hamster
mouse
rat

gerbil

guinea pig

FLYING MAMMAL:
bat

bat

WILD MAMMALS:

badger	giraffe	monkey
bear	hare	rabbit
chimpanzee	hedgehog	rhinoceros
deer	kangaroo	squirrel
elephant	koala	tiger
fox	lion	zebra

bear

elephant

SMALLEST MAMMAL:
pygmy shrew (80 mm including tail)

LARGEST MAMMAL:
blue whale (33 m long)

Mm

a
b
c
d
e
f
g
h
i
j
k
l
n
o
p
q
r
s
t
u
v
w
x
y
z

manage

manage VERB
Someone who **manages** an organization is in charge of it.

be in charge of
"I demand to see whoever **is in charge of** this restaurant," said the customer.

command
Mr Pecksniff **commands** a large department in the store.

control
Our teacher **controls** the class without raising her voice.

direct
The lights broke down and police had to **direct** the traffic.

look after
Mum said she would **look after** the games if somebody else did the food.

run
Our local school needs somebody to **run** the library.

mark NOUN
A **mark** is a small stain on something.

blot
A **blot** appeared mysteriously on Grace's maths work.

smear
Tony washed his hands but there was still a **smear** on his face.

smudge
Becky nearly wept when she found a **smudge** on her drawing.

spot
"Don't worry," said the teacher. "It's only a tiny **spot**."

stain
There was a damp **stain** on the wallpaper where the rain had come in.

meal NOUN
A **meal** is food that people eat, usually at set times during the day.

barbecue
It was a lovely evening, so they had a **barbecue** on the beach.

buffet
Mum arranged a **buffet** so that people could help themselves.

feast
We pitched our tent in the garden and had a late-night **feast**.

picnic
For my birthday, we had a lovely **picnic** beside the river.

snack
Halfway through the morning Toby decided he needed a **snack**.

mean (1) VERB
If you ask what something **means**, you want it explained to you.

indicates
"That sign **indicates** no right turn," said the police officer.

say
Can't you read? That sign **says** you mustn't walk on the grass.

show
The flashing light **shows** the battery is low.

stand for
What does that symbol **stand for**?

mean (2) ADJECTIVE
Someone who is **mean** does not like spending money or sharing.

miserly
Scrooge was a **miserly** person.

selfish
Matt's really **selfish**. He wouldn't give me any of his sweets.

stingy
Some parents are quite **stingy** when it comes to pocket money.

a b c d e f g h i j k l **Mm** n o p q r s t u v w x y z

mean (3) VERB

If you **mean** to do something, you intend to do it.

aim
What do you aim to do when you grow up?

intend
If you intend to be prime minister, you'll have to work harder.

plan
I planned to jump out and surprise him, but it didn't work.

propose
"How do you propose to sort out this mess?" demanded his mum.

meet VERB

If you **meet** someone, you go to the same place at the same time as they do.

come across
We first came across her at a disco.

come upon
They were walking in the mountains when they came upon a troll.

encounter
A hermit lives in this wood, but you are not likely to encounter him.

run across
"You'll never guess who I ran across yesterday," said Joe.

run into
If we go this way we might run into that big dog.

meeting NOUN

A **meeting** is when a group of people meet to talk about particular things.

audience
Angry villagers demanded an urgent audience with the king.

conference
Mr Wilson-Brown is away at a conference of head teachers.

gathering
Outside the school, a gathering of parents discussed the new rules.

get-together
Students who were leaving suggested a get-together the following year.

mend VERB

If you **mend** something that is broken or does not work, you put it right so that it can be used again.

cure
"I know how to cure a broken heart," said the fairy.

darn
Grandma says she used to darn Grandpa's socks to make them last.

fix
Harry fixed the wonky saddle on his bike.

patch
My sister patched her jeans with a bright red square.

repair
The radio was quite easy to repair.

mess

mess (1) NOUN

If you say something is a **mess**, you mean it is very untidy.

chaos Say "**kay**-oss"
She screamed at the **chaos** she found in the kitchen. There was flour everywhere.

clutter
Dad said if I didn't sort out the **clutter**, he'd do it for me.

disorder
It took a long time to get the **disorder** tidied up, but finally everything was back in the right place.

jumble
"Look at that **jumble** of books," said Mum. "Why is it on the floor?"

litter
There was **litter** everywhere.

shambles
After the party the room was a **shambles**.

mess (2) NOUN

If you are in a **mess**, you are in a situation where there are a lot of problems.

fix
The ruby slippers helped Dorothy out of her **fix**.

jam
David was in a **jam** with his maths homework and needed help.

pickle
The wizard got in a **pickle** with his spell.

➔ fine kettle of fish

method NOUN

A **method** is a particular way of doing something.

approach
I think a different **approach** might work a bit better.

manner
Seahorses have an unusual **manner** of giving birth.

plan
Before they began work he explained his **plan** carefully.

system
Barbara has a special **system** for dealing with the mail.

technique
"There is a simple **technique** for sorting out greenfly," said Percy.

way
If you know a better **way** then tell me now.

middle NOUN

The **middle** of something is the part furthest from the edges.

centre
The cat sat in the **centre** of the flowerbed.

heart
The **heart** of the old tree was hollow.

midpoint
By the **midpoint** of the race she was beginning to tire.

thick
William always liked to be in the **thick** of the battle.

mild ADJECTIVE

Someone or something **mild** is gentle and does no harm.

gentle
*The male gorilla had a very **gentle** nature.*

kind
*The witch's tones were **kind**, but they still didn't trust her.*

meek
*"I'm sorry," she said in a **meek** voice. "I didn't mean to hurt you."*

placid
*My great-grandfather has the same **placid** reaction to almost everything.*

pleasant
*She made a **pleasant** comment as she let them through.*

mind (1) NOUN

Your **mind** is your ability to think, together with your memory and all the thoughts you have.

brain
*"I can't get my **brain** round this problem," said Uncle Eddie.*

head
*Emma had plenty of ideas in her **head**. She just needed to transfer them to paper.*

mind (2) VERB

If you **mind** somebody or something, you look after them.

guard
*We let the dog **guard** our ball when we went shopping.*

keep an eye on
*"Please **keep an eye on** my gold," breathed the dragon.*

look after
*Her aunt **looked after** her for the day while her parents were at work.*

take care of
*Caspar the clown **took care of** the performing fleas.*

mind (3) VERB

If you **mind** about something, it worries you or makes you angry.

be bothered
*Daniel **was bothered** about changing schools at the end of the year.*

care
*"I don't **care**," said Jessie. "I've got lots of other friends."*

object to
*The unicorn **objected to** sharing the field with ordinary horses.*

misery NOUN

Misery is great unhappiness.

despair
*Mr Jones was full of **despair** when he lost his job.*

grief
*The swan showed signs of **grief** when its mate died.*

sadness
*We tried to discover the reason for the little boy's **sadness**.*

sorrow
*"Such dreadful **sorrow** is hard to bear," said the wizard.*

unhappiness
*Luckily, her **unhappiness** did not last for more than a day.*

ANTONYM: joy

miss

miss VERB

If you **miss** somebody, you are lonely without them.

feel the loss of
Natalie **felt the loss of** her friend when his family moved.

pine for
Our dog **pined for** my dad while he was away working.

mistake NOUN

A **mistake** is something that is done wrong.

blunder
Tom made a number of **blunders** in the spelling test.

error
"That's excellent," said the teacher. "There are no **errors** at all."

oversight
The king's **oversight** was to forget to invite a fairy godmother.

slip
I only made two small **slips**, but it was enough to make Mum suspicious.

misty ADJECTIVE

If it is **misty**, there are lots of tiny drops of water in the air, and you cannot see very far.

blurred
His eyes were full of tears and everything looked **blurred**.

dim
In the early morning, they watched the **dim** outline of trees becoming clearer.

faint
A **faint** glimmer shone through the clouds.

hazy
The **hazy** sunshine promised a hot day.

indistinct
The figures behind the fountain were **indistinct**, but even through the spray they seemed familiar.

mix VERB

If you **mix** things, you stir them or put them together.

blend
The witch **blended** everything carefully.

combine
If you **combine** blue and yellow you will get green.

mingle
Mum was having a job getting the guests to **mingle** properly.

put together
Holly **put together** flour and water to make a paste.

stir together
Stir together the butter, sugar and eggs in a bowl.

monster NOUN

A **monster** is an imaginary creature that is large and terrifying.

bogey-man
I don't believe in **bogey-men**.

giant
Jack climbed the beanstalk and found a hungry **giant**.

ogre
"You must tell me," said the **ogre**, "why nobody likes me."

troll
A family of **trolls** was having a picnic in the mountains.

move (1) VERB

To **move** means to go to a different place or position.

dart
A mouse **darted** out from a hole under the door.

fly
The bird **flew** away as soon as it saw the farmyard cat.

gallop
A ghostly horse **galloped** through the dark forest.

shoot
Josephine **shot** across the room to save a falling vase.

shuffle
An old man was **shuffling** painfully down the street.

slither
Marcus lifted a stone and a small snake **slithered** out.

stir
Sam **stirred** uneasily in his sleep.

totter
The baby **tottered** a few yards and sat down suddenly.

tremble
Leaves **trembled** in the breeze.

walk
Jake **walked** slowly across the classroom.

zoom
The sports car **zoomed** down the road at great speed.

move (2) VERB

To **move** something means to change its place or position.

bring
"Could you **bring** that little table nearer to me?" asked Gran.

carry
Martin **carried** the television upstairs.

disturb
The professor would not let anyone **disturb** his papers.

drag
Dad **dragged** a huge bag of potatoes into the shed.

fling
Luke **flung** my jacket off his bed.

pull
Ben **pulled** the lever towards him.

push
A toddler was trying to **push** her buggy along the pavement.

take
"Please **take** those disgusting socks away from me!" exclaimed Jane.

move (3) VERB

If you **move**, you change where you are living.

migrate
Some birds **migrate** thousands of miles every year.

move house
They **move house** fairly frequently when their mum changes her job.

a
b
c
d
e
f
g
h
i
j
k
l
Mm
n
o
p
q
r
s
t
u
v
w
x
y
z

music

music NOUN

Music is a pattern of sounds made by people singing or playing instruments.

KINDS OF MUSIC:

classical	pop
country	rap
folk	reggae
jazz	rock
opera	soul

KINDS OF SONGS:

anthem	lullaby
ballad	nursery rhyme
carol	pop song
chant	rap
folk song	round
hymn	

MUSICAL INSTRUMENTS:

bagpipes	guitar	saxophone
banjo	harmonica	sitar
cello	harp	tambourine
clarinet	horn	triangle
didgeridoo	keyboard	trumpet
double bass	oboe	violin
drum	piano	xylophone
flute	recorder	

drum

flute

guitar

harp

keyboard

mysterious (1) ADJECTIVE

Something that is **mysterious** is strange and puzzling.

baffling
Aunt Alice found the disappearance of the cakes baffling.

curious
"What a curious feeling!" said Alice as she began to shrink.

eerie
The house was dark and eerie and full of strange sounds.

ghostly
A tall ghostly figure floated silently across the terrace.

magical
Deep in the centre of the forest was a magical waterfall.

mystifying
A mystifying sound came from beneath the floorboards.

strange
The wizard wore a dark cloak covered in strange designs.

weird
Suddenly the boys came upon a weird door in the wall.

mysterious (2) ADJECTIVE

If someone is being **mysterious**, they are secretive about something.

furtive
A furtive smile appeared on Jasper's face when he worked out the answer.

puzzling
Sarah was very interested in the men's puzzling behaviour.

secretive
Seth was being surprisingly secretive about his plans.

mystery NOUN

A **mystery** is something strange that cannot be explained.

problem
The boys were determined to solve the problem of the curious footprint.

puzzle
It took them a week to find an answer to the puzzle.

question
"The question is," said the detective, "how did the thief get in?"

riddle
The police were baffled by the riddle of the locked room.

secret
Strange writing told of a secret that could never be known.

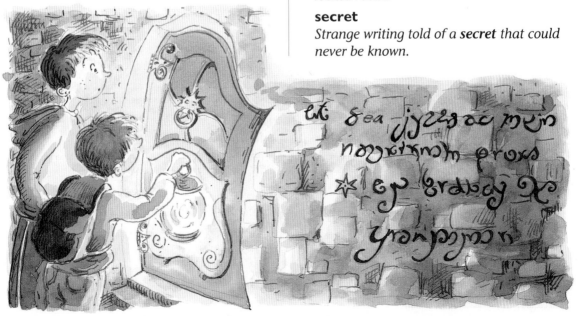

a
b
c
d
e
f
g
h
i
j
k
l
Mm
n
o
p
q
r
s
t
u
v
w
x
y
z

Nn

nasty ADJECTIVE

Something or someone **nasty** is very unpleasant.

disgusting
*The inside of Tom's trainers smelled really **disgusting**.*

horrible
*My sister had a **horrible** rash when she caught measles.*

mean
*Scrooge was a very **mean** person.*

stormy
*Lifeboat crew often have to go out in **stormy** weather.*

unpleasant
*Some animals protect themselves in **unpleasant** ways.*

vile
*A **vile** smell was coming from the kitchen.*

→ loathsome; obnoxious

ANTONYM: pleasant

nervous ADJECTIVE

If you are **nervous**, you are worried about something.

anxious
*He seemed **anxious**, so I asked him what was wrong.*

jumpy
*Our cat was **jumpy** every time we tried to look at the new kittens.*

tense
*My brother gets very **tense** before an exam.*

worried
*Mum was **worried** about cooking for so many people.*

nice (1) ADJECTIVE

You say something is **nice** when you like it.

attractive
*David's girlfriend is very **attractive**.*

beautiful
*Amy had a **beautiful** view of the sunset from her hotel room.*

comfortable
*The inside of Toad's caravan was surprisingly **comfortable**.*

delicious
*That big plate of cakes looks **delicious**.*

enjoyable
*The rabbits had a really **enjoyable** day eating the farmer's cabbages.*

smart
*Mr Magic loved his **smart** new cloak.*

ANTONYM: horrible

nice (2) ADJECTIVE

If you are **nice** to people, you are friendly and kind.

friendly
*I know my dog looks fierce, but he's really very **friendly**.*

helpful
*The people round here are **helpful**.*

kind
*It's **kind** of you to feed the tarantulas while I'm away.*

ANTONYM: nasty

nice (3) ADJECTIVE

If you say the weather is **nice**, it is warm and pleasant.

fine
Our cat will only go out when the weather's fine.

sunny
They went for a picnic on the first sunny day of the year.

warm
It was warm in the garden, so the children played outside.

ANTONYM: bad

noise NOUN

A **noise** is a sound that someone or something makes.

clatter
The clatter of cutlery told them that supper was ready.

commotion
During the commotion, Abhi managed to slip away.

din
The TV was on at full volume and Jackie had to yell above the din.

racket
Dad flung open the door and shouted, "Stop this racket at once!"

row
Jason's motorbike makes an awful row.

noisy ADJECTIVE

Someone or something **noisy** makes loud or unpleasant sounds.

boisterous
Dad complained the party was getting far too boisterous.

deafening
Suddenly there was a deafening clap of thunder.

loud
The boys' game was much too loud.

piercing
She was a nice girl, but they couldn't stand her piercing laugh.

→ ear-splitting

ANTONYM: quiet

normal ADJECTIVE

Something that is **normal** is what you would expect.

average
It's an average sort of house.

everyday
We eat pretty everyday foods, unless we're celebrating something.

ordinary
It was another ordinary day until the ghost appeared.

usual
The sisters were having their usual bedtime argument.

a
b
c
d
e
f
g
h
i
j
k
l
m
Nn
o
p
q
r
s
t
u
v
w
x
y
z

Oo

odd ADJECTIVE

If you say something is **odd**, you mean it is strange or unusual.

funny
*Liam's teacher gave him a **funny** look.*

peculiar
*The sight of blood made her feel **peculiar**.*

strange
*They came to a huge door covered with **strange** pictures.*

weird
*A **weird** sound echoed through the castle and the children froze.*

→ bizarre

offend VERB

If you **offend** someone, you upset them by saying or doing something rude.

annoy
*Claire said she was sorry she had **annoyed** her grandmother.*

displease
*They found it was a mistake to **displease** the ogre.*

insult
*"Don't **insult** your brother," said Mum. "It's not funny."*

upset
*It will **upset** her if you criticize her hairstyle.*

often ADVERB

If something happens **often**, it happens many times.

again and again
*I've thought **again and again** of our lovely holiday in France.*

frequently
*They **frequently** found they'd eaten their lunch by eleven o'clock.*

regularly
*We try to visit the old lady **regularly** because she can't go out.*

repeatedly
*"I've told you **repeatedly**," said his mother, "to wipe your feet on the mat when you come in."*

time after time
Time after time they arrived late.

old (1) ADJECTIVE

Someone who is **old** has lived for a long time.

aged
*In the wood they met an **aged** man with a long white beard.*

elderly
*There were a lot of **elderly** people at the village meeting.*

ANTONYM: young

old (2) ADJECTIVE

Something that is **old** has existed for a long time.

ancient
*"There are a lot of **ancient** buildings in Rome," said Max.*

antique
*One room was full of **antique** clocks, all chiming at once.*

prehistoric
*The museum has a collection of **prehistoric** arrowheads.*

ANTONYM: modern

old (3) ADJECTIVE

Old can mean shabby or worn out.

shabby
*There were only a couple of **shabby** armchairs to sit on.*

tattered
*The wizard's cloak was so **tattered** it looked as if mice had been at it.*

worn out
*Mum complained that her shoes were **worn out**.*

ANTONYM: new

opening NOUN

An **opening** is a hole or space that things or people can go through.

break
*The sun shone briefly through a **break** in the clouds.*

chink
*A **chink** between the curtains allowed a strip of light to escape.*

crack
*Smoke was rising through a **crack** between the floorboards.*

hole
*The boys peered into the garden through a **hole** in the fence.*

slot
*Dad's car keys fell down through a **slot** in the grating.*

space
*There was just a **space** where the door should have been.*

opinion NOUN

An **opinion** is a belief or view.

belief
*It's my **belief** that he is a very talented young artist.*

view
*You should make your **views** known to the head teacher.*

order VERB

If someone **orders** you to do something, they tell you to do it.

command
*The king **commanded** that his jester should be brought to him.*

demand
*"Give me all your money and jewels," **demanded** the highwayman.*

instruct
*Mr Blake **instructed** them to sit absolutely still while he took the register.*

tell
*The doctor **told** Nicky to stay in bed for a week.*

ordinary ADJECTIVE

Something that is **ordinary** is not special in any way.

normal
*It started out as just a **normal** day.*

regular
*His **regular** outfit was T-shirt and jeans.*

routine
*She took the dog on a **routine** walk round the park.*

standard
*They could only afford to buy the **standard** model.*

usual
*"Don't worry," said the doctor. "This is a **usual** complaint for someone your age."*

→ common or garden; run-of-the-mill

ANTONYM: special

a
b
c
d
e
f
g
h
i
j
k
l
m
n
Oo
p
q
r
s
t
u
v
w
x
y
z

Pp

pain NOUN

A **pain** is an unpleasant feeling that you have in part of your body if you have been hurt or are ill.

ache
*She had a dull **ache** in her stomach.*

irritation
*The patchy, red rash was driving him mad with **irritation**.*

soreness
*Mum put a plaster on his grazed knee to help the **soreness**.*

trouble
*His bad tooth was giving him **trouble**.*

twinge
*Grandma complained of a **twinge** in her shoulder and back.*

→ agony; torture

pale ADJECTIVE

Something that is **pale** is without much colour.

colourless
*His favourite T-shirt was **colourless** from endless washing.*

faded
*There were **faded** stripes on the curtains where the sun had caught them.*

pasty
*He has a **pasty** complexion, as if he spends his life indoors.*

sallow
*Her face was **sallow** from a recent illness.*

wan
*She looked tired and **wan** after the journey.*

white
*Chloe turned **white** with shock.*

part NOUN

A **part** is a piece or section of something.

bit
*My favourite **bit** of the book is where he slew the dragon.*

fragment
*They recovered most of the broken bowl, but a **fragment** was still missing.*

piece
*There's one **piece** of the puzzle that remains to be solved.*

portion
*The sloping **portion** of the garden was hard to mow.*

section
*A **section** of the train had to be closed off.*

pattern (1) NOUN

A **pattern** is a diagram or shape used as a guide for making something.

design
*Dad drew up a **design** for the rabbit hutch.*

diagram
*A **diagram** showed how to build the model aircraft.*

plan
*We followed the **plan** exactly but the table still looked odd.*

stencil
*The pack included a **stencil** and paint for the lettering.*

template
*Hannah pinned the **template** of a skirt on the material and cut round it.*

pattern (2) NOUN

A **pattern** can be a design of repeated shapes.

arrangement
*Heather's new dress was blue with an **arrangement** of white flowers.*

design
*The wizard's cloak was covered in a **design** of stars and moons.*

pause NOUN

A **pause** is a short period when something stops.

break
*There was a **break** in the conversation when a stranger walked in.*

delay
*The clown announced a **delay** in his act while he hunted for his shoes.*

gap
*Sometimes TV programmes have **gaps** for advertisements.*

halt
*The games teacher signalled a **halt** in the race. Two children were running in the wrong direction.*

intermission
*The show started with advertisements, then there was an **intermission** before the animal film began.*

interruption
*Fire practice created an **interruption** in the lesson.*

interval
*Spencer went to get an ice cream in the **interval** between the acts.*

rest
*Mel demanded a **rest** before pressing on with the hike.*

peace NOUN

Peace is a feeling of quiet and calm.

calm
*Storm clouds were threatening to disturb the **calm** of the afternoon.*

quiet
*The **quiet** of the lane was a relief after the noisy motorway.*

silence
*Not even birdsong interrupted the perfect **silence** of the wood.*

stillness
*A screech from an owl shattered the **stillness** of the night.*

tranquillity
*The family moved to the country in search of **tranquillity**.*

persuade VERB

If someone **persuades** you to do something you did not want to do, you agree because they give you a good reason.

coax
*We **coaxed** Dad to take us to the zoo by saying it was educational.*

entice
*Raffy **enticed** the rabbit back into her hutch by putting a carrot in it.*

sway
*My sister is often **swayed** by clever advertisements on TV.*

tempt
*Henry **tempted** his brother to come by promising he'd see fox cubs.*

urge
*The head teacher **urged** us to consider after-school activities.*

pester

pester VERB

If you **pester** someone, you keep bothering them.

annoy
Can't you go and annoy someone else?

badger
Amy's little brother badgered her until she agreed to play with him.

bother
Don't bother Grandma now. She's trying to sleep.

nag
Sam kept nagging his dad to get him a new bike.

plague
They took a picnic to the river but were soon plagued by mosquitoes.

→ get on someone's nerves; drive someone up the wall

pick (1) VERB

To **pick** means to choose.

choose
We chose Kaitlin as our captain.

decide on
Timothy couldn't decide on a name for his ginger kitten.

select
The king selected the bravest knight to be his champion.

pick (2) VERB

When you **pick** flowers or fruit, you take them off the plant.

collect
The sisters went into the orchard to collect ripe plums.

cut
Nadia cut roses for the jug in the hall.

gathered
We went out to gather blackberries.

pluck
He tested each pear before plucking it from the tree.

picture (1) NOUN

A **picture** is a drawing, painting or photograph.

KINDS OF PICTURES:

cartoon	painting
collage	photograph
diagram	portrait
drawing	poster
map	print
mosaic	sketch
mural	

cartoon

diagram

map

picture (2) VERB

If you **picture** something in your mind, you can imagine it.

imagine
Katherine could imagine her friend's surprise when she opened the present.

see
He could see what was going to happen.

visualize
They tried to visualize what the new teacher would look like.

piece NOUN

A **piece** is a part of something.

bit
A **bit** of pie fell on the floor and the dog gobbled it up.

lump
Lumps of clay were lying on the table where the sculptor was working.

scrap
She was sewing together **scraps** of material to make a patchwork quilt.

shred
Our naughty puppy ripped the rug to **shreds**.

slab
The builder used large **slabs** of stone to make the patio.

slice
Nathan cut himself a **slice** of cake.

pile NOUN

A **pile** is a lot of things, such as books, which have been put one on top of the other.

heap
She nearly tripped over a **heap** of dirty washing left on the floor.

hoard
In the cave, they came upon a **hoard** of gold and silver.

mound
There was a curious **mound** of stones beside the path.

mountain
People had left a **mountain** of things for the jumble sale.

stack
A **stack** of books lay beside his chair, waiting to be read.

place (1) NOUN

A **place** is a building or area.

area
Uncle Peter wants to move to an **area** with lots of fields and trees.

district
This **district** doesn't have many shops.

house
It's an ordinary sort of **house**.

neighbourhood
Sasha and her family live in a very friendly **neighbourhood**.

spot
The barge was moored at a peaceful **spot** on the river.

place (2) VERB

If you **place** something somewhere, you put it there.

lay
Gwendolin **laid** the injured fairy in a cobweb hammock.

leave
"**Leave** the groceries by the back door, please," said Lesley.

plant
Her grandma **planted** hollyhocks next to the wall.

put
He **put** a deckchair in the shade of a tree.

set out
Mole and Ratty **set out** their picnic beside the river.

plain

plain (1) ADJECTIVE

Something that is **plain** is simple with no decoration.

basic
*The furniture at the hostel was **basic**, but quite comfortable.*

modest
*Hitomi loved his hillside home even though it was very **modest**.*

ordinary
*It was an **ordinary** wooden table with no decoration.*

simple
*Dan only wanted a **simple** jam sandwich for tea.*

plain (2) ADJECTIVE

Plain can mean clear and easy to see.

clear
*The meaning of her words was **clear**.*

obvious
*It was **obvious** that Tom was upset. His bottom lip was quivering.*

plan (1) NOUN

If you have a **plan**, you have thought of a way of doing something.

idea
*Sam had an **idea** that was sure to work. His bike would be mended in no time.*

method
*The team needed a different **method** if it was going to succeed.*

scheme
*Emma thought of a clever **scheme** to raise money.*

system
*They all agreed the **system** was a failure.*

plan (2) NOUN

A **plan** is a detailed drawing of something that is to be made.

design
*They loved the **design** for the robot.*

diagram
*"It's a spaceship **diagram**," said Ian.*

drawing
*The file contained a **drawing** that showed part of the new car's engine.*

layout
*Leonie studied the **layout** before she started building her model.*

plan (3) VERB

If you **plan** what you are going to do, you decide how to do it.

aim
*Emilio **aimed** to be the new team captain.*

arrange
*"The spell works at dawn," said the witch. "You'd better **arrange** to be out."*

design
*The teacher **designed** tests to show each child's abilities.*

intend
*Captain Fantastic **intended** to land on the planet Jupiter.*

organize
*Mr Lewis **organized** a sack race for the parents.*

think about
*"It's no good rushing in," said Amanda. "We need to **think about** this."*

play (1) VERB

When you **play**, you spend time doing things you enjoy.

amuse yourself
"Please amuse yourselves quietly while Grandpa has a rest," said Gran.

have fun
The cousins had fun in the paddling pool all afternoon.

romp about
Our garden is the sort of place where you can romp about safely.

play (2) VERB

When one person or team **plays** another, they take part in a game and each side tries to win.

challenge
He was good at tennis and was prepared to challenge anybody in his group.

compete against
Blues are competing against yellows in the next race.

take on
The girls' team is ready to take on the boys at football.

play (3) NOUN

A **play** is a story that is acted on the stage, or on radio or television.

comedy
There was a really funny comedy on television last night.

drama
Mum likes to hear radio dramas, especially if they have happy endings.

performance
Our class put on a terrific performance at the end of term.

show
On my birthday we're going to the theatre to see a show.

tragedy
It's a tragedy where everybody ends up getting killed.

pleasant (1) ADJECTIVE

Something that is **pleasant** is enjoyable or attractive.

agreeable
Mum painted the kitchen an agreeable shade of blue.

charming
It was a charming beach far away from the crowds.

delightful
Uncle Dave said they had a delightful view of the countryside from the hotel.

enjoyable
We spent an enjoyable afternoon fishing for shrimps in rock pools.

refreshing
After their walk, the girls cooled down in the refreshing breeze.

satisfying
They finished the day with a satisfying meal at the local restaurant.

pleasant (2) ADJECTIVE

A person who is **pleasant** is friendly and likeable.

amiable
I know you don't like her, but she always seems amiable to me.

cheerful
Everyone at the supermarket is cheerful and willing to help.

friendly
A friendly woman with a baby told them where to find the park.

plot

plot NOUN

A **plot** is a secret plan made by a group of people.

conspiracy

The pirate captain was sure there was a ***conspiracy*** *against him.*

plan

Guy Fawkes worked out a ***plan*** *to blow up the Houses of Parliament.*

scheme

The Sheriff of Nottingham thought up a ***scheme*** *to trap Robin Hood.*

poetry NOUN

Poetry is writing in which the lines have a rhythm and sometimes rhyme.

poem

They were asked to write ***poems*** *about something that interested them.*

rhyme

Jessie was good at thinking up funny ***rhymes*** *to entertain her friends.*

verse

The author handed out books of ***verse*** *for the children to look at.*

KINDS OF POETRY:

acrostic	haiku
ballad	jingle
blank verse	limerick
calligram	narrative poem
cinquain	nursery rhyme
concrete poem	ode
couplet	rap
elegy	shape poem
epic	sonnet
free verse	tanka

point NOUN

The **point** of something is the purpose or meaning it has.

aim

The main ***aim*** *of a thesaurus is to help you find words with similar meanings.*

goal

A leaflet explained that the ***goal*** *was to raise money for Children In Need.*

object

Nick's main ***object*** *in life was football.*

purpose

She couldn't see much ***purpose*** *in computer games.*

poke VERB

If you **poke** someone, you quickly push them with your finger or a sharp object.

jab

"Don't speak to me like that!" he shouted, ***jabbing*** *her shoulder.*

nudge

Ranjit giggled and ***nudged*** *his friend in the ribs with an elbow.*

prod

Esther ***prodded*** *the bulge in her little brother's pocket. "What have you got in there?" she asked.*

polite ADJECTIVE

Someone who is **polite** has good manners and thinks about other people's feelings.

civil

You don't have to like her, but you can at least be ***civil***.

courteous

He was a ***courteous*** *man who always raised his hat to a woman.*

respectful

She was brought up to be ***respectful*** *to older people.*

well-mannered

"It's nice to see such a ***well-mannered*** *little boy," she said.*

poor ADJECTIVE

Someone who is **poor** has very little money and few possessions.

broke INFORMAL

*Alex says he's too **broke** to go out with us.*

deprived

*This is a very **deprived** area.*

hard up INFORMAL

*If you're so **hard up**, how can you afford those trainers?*

pour VERB

To **pour** means to flow quickly and in large amounts.

gush

*Blood **gushed** from the dragon's wounds.*

run

*The heavy rain **ran** down the gutters.*

spill

*Water **spilled** everywhere as Jack dropped his bucket.*

stream

*Tears **streamed** down Rachel's face.*

→ bucket down; come down in torrents; rain cats and dogs

power NOUN

The **power** of something, such as the wind or the sea, is its strength.

force

*The **force** of the wind blew a branch across the road.*

strength

*Trees near our cottage could not stand against the **strength** of the storm.*

private ADJECTIVE

If something is **private**, only a few people know about it.

confidential

*Don't tell anyone else. It's **confidential**.*

quiet

*Clare had her own **quiet** place at the end of the garden.*

secluded

*The beach was **secluded**, so they could swim in peace.*

secret

*Sean took them in through a **secret** door.*

solitary

*The wizard lived in a **solitary** cottage, tucked away in the wood.*

problem (1) NOUN

A **problem** is something that is difficult.

complication

*"There's a **complication**, I'm afraid," he said. "There aren't any boats to take you to your holiday island."*

difficulty

*"We can soon sort out that little **difficulty**," said Sophie.*

trouble

*"If you have any **trouble** finding your size, just ask," said the shop assistant.*

→ can of worms; hard nut to crack

problem (2) NOUN

A **problem** can also be something like a puzzle that you have to work out.

brain-teaser

*Kate spent many happy hours solving all sorts of **brain-teasers**.*

puzzle

*Dad's brilliant at crossword **puzzles**.*

question

*Nobody could do the last **question**.*

riddle

*They had to think very hard about the **riddle** before they knew what to do.*

promise

promise VERB

If you **promise** to do something, you mean you really will do it.

assure
Graham **assured** us he'd have the car ready by Friday.

give your word
Jessica **gave her word** she'd be home by five o'clock.

guarantee
The shop assistant **guaranteed** the colours wouldn't run.

vow
Caroline **vowed** she wouldn't tell anyone the secret.

→ cross your heart; swear

proper ADJECTIVE

The **proper** thing is the one that is correct or most suitable.

apt
It was hard to find an **apt** description for the wizard's strange behaviour.

correct
You must fill the space in each sentence with the **correct** word.

fitting
The applause was a **fitting** end to such a wonderful play.

right
I'd like to know the **right** name for my new plant.

suitable
We don't have a **suitable** tool to deal with that job.

protect VERB

To **protect** someone or something is to prevent them from being harmed.

defend
He's always ready to **defend** his little brother in the playground.

guard
Our dog **guards** the house by barking at anyone it doesn't know.

look after
"You must **look after** your hamster when the cat's around," said Mum, "or he'll get eaten."

shelter
A shed in the field **shelters** the donkey in bad weather.

shield
Alice's umbrella **shielded** her from the pouring rain.

proud ADJECTIVE

If you feel **proud**, you feel glad about something you have done, or about something that belongs to you.

glad
Our team was **glad** to win the cup after all that hard work.

gratified
The actors were **gratified** when the audience rose to its feet and cheered.

honoured
Uncle Jim says he is **honoured** to be chosen as a judge at the pet show.

pleased
Rosie's parents were so **pleased** when she came top of the class.

pull VERB

When you **pull** something, you hold it firmly and move it towards you.

drag
*Sebastian **dragged** out his train set from the cupboard.*

draw
*"**Draw** that chair nearer to the fire and keep warm," said Gran.*

haul
*Daisy **hauled** a jumper from her bag.*

heave
*Between them they managed to **heave** the sack into the garage.*

tow
*The car broke down and we had to get a truck to **tow** us home.*

tug
*Simon **tugged** as hard as he could, but his friend was stuck.*

ANTONYM: push

pure ADJECTIVE

Something that is **pure** is not mixed with anything else.

clean
*It is much healthier and more pleasant to breathe **clean** air.*

clear
*They drank **clear** water that bubbled up from the spring.*

natural
*Ruth liked the feel of **natural** silk against her skin.*

real
*Mum always buys **real** fruit juices for us to drink at break.*

unmixed
*When she saw her old friend she felt **unmixed** joy.*

unpolluted
*Far from the motorway, the atmosphere was **unpolluted**.*

push VERB

When you **push** something, you press it hard.

force
*There was a huge crowd and the children had to **force** their way to the front.*

poke
*Bertha **poked** a stick in the sand.*

press
***Press** the doorbell so Charlie knows we have arrived.*

thrust
*Sir Jasper **thrust** his sword into the dragon's belly.*

ANTONYM: pull

put VERB

When you **put** something somewhere, you move it there.

arrange
*Mum **arranged** the flowers in a vase.*

dump
*Stephen came in and **dumped** his bag in the hall.*

lay
*She **laid** the baby in his cot and sang a quiet lullaby.*

leave
*They **left** newspapers and glass bottles in the blue box to be recycled.*

pile
*Matilda **piled** the library books beside her bedroom chair.*

place
*Trevor **placed** the insect on his hand for the others to see.*

set out
*They **set out** the chess pieces on the board.*

Qq

quality NOUN

The **quality** of something is how good or bad it is, compared with other things of the same kind.

excellence
*It was a chance to show the **excellence** of their work.*

grade
*King Henry's tailor always used cloth of the finest **grade**.*

standard
*"I expect your writing to be of a high **standard**," said the teacher.*

value
*Things from that greengrocer are always good **value**.*

quarrel NOUN

A **quarrel** is an angry argument.

argument
*I've just had an **argument** with my friend and she won.*

disagreement
*There was a **disagreement** about the seating in class.*

fight
*My brothers had a **fight** over the train set.*

row
*The washing-up often leads to a **row** in our house.*

squabble
*The girls had a silly **squabble** then quickly made friends again.*

question VERB

If you **question** someone or something, you try to find something out.

ask
*The police officer **asked** him about his movements that night.*

interrogate
*Spencer **interrogated** everyone who might have seen his lost guinea pig.*

probe into
*They decided to **probe into** the reasons for her behaviour.*

quiz
*Meredith **quizzed** her about her job as a nanny.*

quick (1) ADJECTIVE

Someone or something that is **quick** moves very fast.

brisk
*The family went for a **brisk** walk through the park.*

fast
*Albert was a surprisingly **fast** elephant.*

hurried
*I could tell by her **hurried** greeting that she didn't have time to chat.*

rapid
*With a **rapid** movement, the conjuror made the watch vanish.*

speedy
*The mouse found his cage door open and made a **speedy** exit.*

➔ like lightning; in a flash

ANTONYM: **slow**

quick (2) ADJECTIVE

Something that is **quick** lasts only a short time.

brief

We had a **brief** talk in the playground.

hurried

They had a **hurried** meal before going to the cinema.

swift

The robot read a whole page with a **swift** movement of its eye.

ANTONYM: long

quick (3) ADJECTIVE

Quick can mean happening without any delay.

prompt

"No, there's nobody here," came the **prompt** reply.

sudden

The cat made a **sudden** jump and caught a mouse by its tail.

quiet (1) ADJECTIVE

Someone or something that is **quiet** makes little noise or no noise at all.

low

"I think he's coming now," said Rupert in a **low** voice.

shy

Vanessa was a **shy** little girl.

silent

The teacher glared at them. "You must be **silent** for at least two minutes."

soft

There was a **soft** sound of purring coming from the bed.

timid

"Don't be so **timid**," said Zina. "Speak up for yourself."

→ quiet as a mouse

ANTONYM: noisy

quiet (2) ADJECTIVE

Quiet means peaceful.

calm

Things soon became **calm** again after the boys' squabble.

hushed

The whole room was **hushed** as the head teacher began to speak.

peaceful

Mum had a lovely **peaceful** time when the children went back to school.

quite (1) ADVERB

Quite can mean rather.

fairly

She could run **fairly** fast.

rather

The sea was **rather** choppy.

quite (2) ADVERB

Quite can mean completely.

absolutely

We were **absolutely** worn out when we arrived home.

completely

Are you **completely** finished now?

fully

The dragon said he **fully** understood the problem he'd caused.

Rr

ready ADJECTIVE

If someone or something is **ready**, they are properly prepared for something.

organized
"Everything was **organized** for the picnic when it began to pour with rain," explained Auntie Anne.

prepared
Hamish wasn't sure he was **prepared** to say his lines.

ripe
The fruit had to be **ripe** before they would eat it.

set
Ten minutes later, they were all **set** to go to the park.

real (1) ADJECTIVE

Something that is **real** is true. It is not imaginary.

actual
The **actual** story of what happened was quite different.

genuine
Her tales of the mysterious figure in the wood are **genuine**.

true
They watched a film that was based on a **true** adventure.

ANTONYM: imaginary

real (2) ADJECTIVE

You can say **real** when you mean the thing itself and not a copy.

authentic
My great-grandpa has an **authentic** air-force jacket.

genuine
The man told them the painting was a **genuine** Rembrandt.

true
She tried to hide her **true** feelings about the boy.

ANTONYM: fake

reptile NOUN

A **reptile** is a cold-blooded animal with a scaly skin. Female reptiles lay eggs.

SOME REPTILES:

alligator	lizard
crocodile	snake
dinosaur (extinct)	tortoise
gecko	turtle

alligator

lizard

snake

turtle

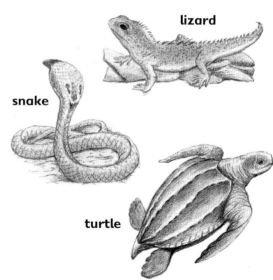

rest (1) VERB

When you **rest**, you sit or lie down and keep still for a while.

put your feet up
Grandma puts her feet up after lunch.

relax
At the weekend Alex liked to relax and read his book.

sit down
Sabrina said if she didn't sit down she'd fall down.

take it easy
"Well done," said the teacher. "Now you can take it easy for a while."

rest (2) NOUN

A **rest** is a period of time when you do not work.

break
Take a break now, and come back here in ten minutes.

holiday
Dad says he could do with a long holiday.

pause
After a short pause she continued reading the story.

rest (3) NOUN

The **rest** is all the things in a group that are left.

leftovers
Some of the food vanished at the party. We put the leftovers in the fridge.

others
Emma finished her work and went home. The others had to stay.

remainder
Put a deposit on the bike now, and pay the remainder when you collect it.

right (1) ADJECTIVE

If something is **right**, it is correct.

accurate
Your measurements must be accurate, or it won't fit.

correct
If the information is correct, we'll take off at 11 o'clock.

exact
It's no good guessing. I need to know the exact answer.

spot-on INFORMAL
Harriet's maths work was always spot-on.

true
It was an interesting story, but William wasn't sure it was true.

ANTONYM: **wrong**

right (2) ADJECTIVE

Right also means the most suitable.

appropriate
He asked what would be the appropriate thing to do.

ideal
They all thought Ashley would be the ideal team leader.

proper
Robin spent ages finding the proper words to describe his hero.

suitable
The tiny flat wasn't suitable as a home for a large dog.

rise

rise (1) VERB

If something **rises**, it moves upwards.

ascend
*The lift **ascended** with great speed.*

climb
*Next year, the number of children in the school will **climb** rapidly.*

get to your feet
*They all **got to their feet** and cheered.*

get up
*"What time do you **get up** in the morning?" asked Sophia.*

soar
*We watched the kite **soar** into the sky.*

stand up
*Edward had to **stand up** when his name was called.*

take off
*The plane **took off** and disappeared above the clouds.*

rise (2) VERB

To **rise** can mean to increase.

go up
*My pocket money will **go up** next week, I hope.*

grow
*TV chiefs expected viewing numbers to **grow** quickly.*

improve
*Pass rates in the test have **improved** again this year.*

increase
*At the moment, prices are still **increasing**.*

ANTONYM: fall

rough (1) ADJECTIVE

If something is **rough**, the surface is uneven and not smooth.

bumpy
*Our car jerked all over the place on the **bumpy** road.*

craggy
*They gazed in dismay at the **craggy** mountainside above them.*

rocky
*A lighthouse can signal warnings of a **rocky** coastline.*

uneven
*The track was **uneven** and she stumbled several times.*

ANTONYM: smooth

rough (2) ADJECTIVE

Rough can mean difficult or unpleasant.

difficult
*Miss Honey had quite a **difficult** life with her aunt.*

hard
*Charles Dickens wrote about **hard** times in Victorian England.*

tough
*A fisherman's job can be very **tough**.*

uncomfortable
*We had an **uncomfortable** ride in a donkey cart.*

unpleasant
*Cinderella had to do all the **unpleasant** work in the house.*

ANTONYM: easy

rough (3) ADJECTIVE

A **rough** estimate is not meant to be exact.

approximate
*Work out the **approximate** size of the school playground.*

estimated
*The **estimated** cost of the building sounded reasonable.*

sketchy
*Kylie had only a **sketchy** idea of how the thing worked.*

vague
*Charles could give only a **vague** description of the man.*

ANTONYM: exact

ruin VERB

To **ruin** something means to spoil it completely.

demolish
*They are **demolishing** a big house to make way for flats.*

destroy
*Trees fell in a violent storm and **destroyed** a beautiful garden.*

smash
*A car swerved off the road and **smashed** the fence.*

wreck
*Some large animals trampled on our tent and **wrecked** it.*

run (1) VERB

When you **run**, you move quickly, leaving the ground during each stride.

bolt
*The horse **bolted**, dragging the cart with it.*

dash
*"Is that the right time?" asked Rosemary. "I must **dash**."*

gallop
*The pony **galloped** across the common.*

hurry
*"There's no need to **hurry**," said Danny.*

race
*They had to **race** to the sweetshop before it closed.*

scamper
*Mice **scampered** across the floor of the old water mill.*

run (2) VERB

Someone who **runs** something, like a school or country, is in charge of it.

be in charge of
*The head teacher **is in charge of** our school. She's called Ms Johns.*

lead
*We need another person to **lead** our swimming group.*

look after
*Jamal was asked to **look after** the stationery cupboard.*

manage
*Clare's dad **manages** the supermarket in our town.*

a b c d e f g h i j k l m n o p q **Rr** s t u v w x y z

a
b
c
d
e
f
g
h
i
j
k
l
m
n
o
p
q
r
Ss
t
u
v
w
x
y
z

Ss

sad (1) ADJECTIVE

If you are **sad**, you are unhappy because something has happened that you do not like.

dejected
*They all felt **dejected** when the birthday party was cancelled.*

gloomy
*Eeyore was a very **gloomy** animal.*

miserable
*I tried to cheer up my big sister when she felt **miserable**.*

tearful
*Ranjit was **tearful** when his budgie died.*

unhappy
*I had never seen James look so **unhappy**.*

ANTONYM: happy

sad (2) ADJECTIVE

Things that are **sad** make you feel unhappy.

depressing
*Dad didn't like the film. He said it was too **depressing**.*

disappointing
*It was **disappointing** when the storybook prince and princess didn't get married.*

dismal
*It was an exciting game but the final score was **dismal**.*

dreadful
*There was news of a **dreadful** loss of life in the earthquake.*

tragic
*Harry Potter learned of the **tragic** death of his parents.*

safe (1) ADJECTIVE

If you are **safe**, you are not in any danger.

out of harm's way
*"Luckily, everyone was **out of harm's way** when the floods came," explained the town spokesperson.*

protected
*Wildlife is **protected** in nature reserves across the country.*

secure
*Charlie loved being tucked up in bed. It made him feel **secure**.*

undamaged
*Emily picked up the crying baby. "It's okay, you're **undamaged**," she said.*

unhurt
*Mehmet crawled out from the wreckage, stood up, and was surprised to find he was **unhurt**.*

→ safe and sound; safe as houses

safe (2) ADJECTIVE

If something is **safe**, it does not cause harm or danger.

harmless
*They thought the snake was poisonous, but it was **harmless**.*

pure
*A scientist tested the water to make sure it was **pure**.*

unpolluted
*Anna walked deep into the woods where the air was **unpolluted**.*

ANTONYM: dangerous

save

satisfactory ADJECTIVE

satisfactory ADJECTIVE

Something that is **satisfactory** is good enough for its purpose.

acceptable
The king seemed to find the jester's silly jokes acceptable.

adequate
"Portions of food are rather small in our canteen," said Gregory, "but they're just about adequate."

all right
"I suppose the holiday was all right," Melek admitted.

good enough
"Your excuse is not good enough," said the teacher. "I do not want you to be late again."

passable
Silvester produced a passable portrait of his friend.

tolerable
She spent a tolerable afternoon watching the cricket.

satisfy VERB

To **satisfy** someone means to give them what they want.

content
The cat contented herself with a patch of sun to lie in.

fill
His new friend filled his need for company of his own age.

please
You can always please Mum with chocolates on her birthday.

save (1) VERB

If you **save** someone or something, you help them escape from harm or danger.

free
They managed to free a bird that was caught in some netting.

liberate
Kylie was tangled in brambles but her mum soon liberated her.

release
Theodore released his hamster from the cat's jaws.

rescue
A dog rescued its owners by barking when the fire started.

salvage
The shipwrecked sailor managed to salvage a number of tools.

save (2) VERB

If you **save** money, you gradually collect it by not spending it all.

hoard
The king hoarded his wealth while the courtiers went around in rags.

keep
Auntie Mavis likes to keep a bit of cash for special treats.

put aside
I put aside some of my pocket money every week.

reserve
Mrs Jones always reserves some of her pension in case she needs it later.

say

say VERB

When you **say** something, you speak words.

announce
*The giraffe **announced** the winner of the knobbly knees contest.*

answer
*Esther called, "Who's there?" "It's only me," **answered** Joe.*

ask
*"Can you come to my party?" **asked** Ben. "We're having a cake."*

claim
*Abdul **claimed** there was a monster under his bed.*

complain
*"I haven't any friends left," **complained** the dragon.*

confess
*"I'm not really brave," **confessed** the stuntman. "I'm scared of beetles."*

emphasize
*"You must be home by midnight," **emphasized** Cinderella's fairy godmother.*

exclaim
*"Oh no!" she **exclaimed**. "My hair has turned green!"*

hint
*Grandma **hinted** she'd like a skateboard for her birthday.*

hiss
*"S-stay here where I can s-see you," **hissed** the snake.*

insist
*The king **insisted** he was going to sing a song he'd composed.*

laugh
*"You can't catch me," **laughed** Sam, and swung up into a tree.*

murmur
*"I'm rather timid," **murmured** the fairy.*

promise
***Promise** you won't bring that rat into school again.*

pronounce
*She **pronounced** her name clearly.*

read out
*The princess **read out** her piece and everyone clapped.*

recite
*The children fell about laughing as Tom **recited** his limericks.*

remark
*"I may be slow," **remarked** the tortoise, "but at least I get there."*

repeat
*Sunita had to **repeat** her question twice.*

reply
*"What are you supposed to be?" asked the judge. "An astronaut," **replied** Tim.*

snap
*"Go away," he **snapped**. "I'm busy."*

stammer
*"H-h-help!" **stammered** the boy. "It's a spaceship!"*

scarce ADJECTIVE

Something that is **scarce** is not often found.

few and far between
*Buses are **few and far between** in this part of the world.*

in short supply
*In some countries, food and medicines are **in short supply**.*

rare
*Birds of prey are becoming quite **rare** in some areas.*

thin on the ground
*Volunteers for this cleaning project are a bit **thin on the ground**.*

uncommon
*Only a few years ago computers were **uncommon**, but now lots of people have them at home.*

unusual
*"That type of stamp is **unusual**," said the collector. "I've only seen one before."*

scare VERB

Someone or something that **scares** you makes you feel frightened.

alarm
*The expression on the wizard's face **alarmed** them.*

frighten
*The wild wood **frightened** mole.*

startle
*Suddenly, a barn owl screeched and **startled** him.*

terrify
*The ogre **terrified** everybody.*

scatter VERB

If you **scatter** things, you throw or drop a lot of them all over an area.

fling
*The children **flung** the papers in the air in excitement.*

litter
*Clothes were **littered** all over Lewis's bedroom floor.*

sow
*As fast as Grandpa **sowed** his seeds, the birds gobbled them up.*

spread
*"**Spread** the corn evenly," she said, "so that all the chickens get some."*

sprinkle
*Mum carefully **sprinkled** drops of water on the seedlings.*

scrape (1) VERB

If you **scrape** something, you rub a rough or sharp object over it.

scratch
*Daniel accidentally **scratched** the table with his model car.*

scuff
*Libby tripped and **scuffed** her new shoes on the path.*

scrape (2) VERB

If something **scrapes** against something else, it makes a harsh noise.

grate
*The hinges **grated** as the old iron gate swung open.*

grind
*Farmer Brown's cartwheels **ground** against the gravel.*

rasp
*Stefan's hand **rasped** across the stubble on his chin.*

squeak
*A knife **squeaked** on the plate and set his teeth on edge.*

scream VERB

If you **scream**, you shout or cry in a loud high-pitched voice.

howl

*Bernard **howled** with pain when the pony stood on his foot.*

screech

*"How dare you ruin my spell!" **screeched** the witch.*

shriek

*We **shrieked** with laughter at his jokes.*

squeal

*The piglet **squealed** when they picked it up.*

yell

*"Help!" he **yelled**. "I've fallen in a ditch."*

search VERB

If you **search** for something, you try to find it.

cast around

*Philip **cast around** for an excuse not to go on the trip.*

comb

*They **combed** the field, looking for her missing purse.*

hunt

*Ben's football boots couldn't be found, though he **hunted** high and low.*

look

*Jessie **looked** everywhere, but there was no sign of her book.*

scour

*The dog **scoured** the whole garden until he found his bone.*

secret ADJECTIVE

Something **secret** is known about by only a small number of people.

hidden

*Joe had a **hidden** den in the bushes at the bottom of the garden.*

out-of-the-way

*They knew an **out-of-the-way** place where they could hold their meetings.*

private

*Her diary was **private** and nobody was allowed to read it.*

secluded

*The cottage had its own **secluded** beach.*

→ cloak and dagger

see (1) VERB

If you **see** something, you are looking at it or you notice it.

glimpse

*Out of the corner of his eye, Gary **glimpsed** a tiny creature.*

notice

*"Have you **noticed** my new trousers?" Mandy demanded.*

observe

*Astronomers **observed** strange marks on the planet's surface.*

spot

*The boys **spotted** Lauren creeping along behind the bushes.*

watch

*The wolf **watched** Little Red Riding Hood walk through the forest.*

see (2) VERB

To **see** something also means to understand it.

follow
*They couldn't quite **follow** what the teacher was trying to say.*

get
*"I don't **get** the joke," said Henry.*

grasp
*She quickly **grasped** what was going on.*

realize
*Alice **realized** that something very curious was happening.*

understand
*Logan was the first to **understand** how the plan would work.*

seize VERB

If you **seize** something, you grab it firmly.

clutch
*The train stopped suddenly. Angela almost fell and had to **clutch** a seat.*

grab
*Rashid **grabbed** his bag and sprinted for the bus.*

grasp
*The old lady **grasped** Katherine's arm and asked for help.*

snatch
*A robber tried to **snatch** her purse, but she held on tightly.*

sensible ADJECTIVE

People who are **sensible** know what is the right thing to do.

down-to-earth
*My Auntie Hyacinth must be the most **down-to-earth** person I know.*

practical
*When you get in a muddle, you need someone **practical** to help you out.*

reasonable
*He's always so **reasonable** you can't argue with him.*

sound
*Most of her ideas are pretty **sound**.*

wise
*It might be **wise** to get home before it begins to rain.*

ANTONYM: foolish

sensitive (1) ADJECTIVE

If you are **sensitive**, you are easily upset about something.

easily upset
*She is **easily upset** when people won't eat her cooking.*

thin-skinned
*Kim is very **thin-skinned**, and cries easily.*

touchy
*My dad's rather **touchy** about the dent in his car.*

sensitive (2) ADJECTIVE

If something is **sensitive**, it is easily affected.

delicate
*The fairy's wings were far too **delicate** to touch.*

fine
*The baby has to stay out of the sun because of her **fine** skin.*

responsive
*Some flowers are **responsive** to daylight. They close at night.*

a b c d e f g h i j k l m n o p q r **Ss** t u v w x y z

separate

separate ADJECTIVE

If two things are **separate**, they are not connected.

detached
*My friend lives in a house that's **detached** from the one next door.*

divided
*A low fence keeps the play area **divided** from the rest of the garden.*

isolated
*The children with measles were kept **isolated** from the others.*

serious (1) ADJECTIVE

Things that are **serious** are very bad and worrying.

bad
*Flooding was particularly **bad** in low-lying areas.*

dreadful
*The storm caused **dreadful** problems for ships at sea.*

severe
*In some countries there is a **severe** shortage of food.*

terrible
*There was a **terrible** accident on the motorway near here.*

worrying
*The colonel reported a **worrying** lack of supplies at the camp.*

serious (2) ADJECTIVE

Serious can mean important and needing careful thought.

difficult
*We need to think carefully about this. It could be **difficult**.*

important
*The head teacher had an **important** announcement to make.*

no laughing matter
*They soon found that missing school was **no laughing matter**.*

serious (3) ADJECTIVE

Someone who is **serious** is sincere about something.

genuine
*The man made Dad a **genuine** offer for the car.*

in earnest
*The coach was **in earnest** about our need to practise.*

sincere
*Daisy had a **sincere** wish to help old people when she grew up.*

serious (4) ADJECTIVE

People who are **serious** are often quiet and do not laugh very much.

grave
*The wizard looked **grave**. "I can't help," he admitted.*

solemn
*Tommy was a **solemn** little boy, but we made him laugh.*

thoughtful
*She had a **thoughtful** look on her face.*

settle VERB

If you **settle** something, you decide or arrange it.

agree
*"We need to **agree** a date for the first rehearsal," said Rachel.*

decide
*Have you **decided** where the party's going to be?*

resolve
*The captain is still trying to **resolve** the problem of the stowaway.*

shake (1) VERB

If something or someone **shakes**, they move from side to side or up and down.

quake
*The dragon stood **quaking** as the knight drew his sword.*

shiver
*Simon **shivered** with cold and wished he'd brought his jacket.*

shudder
*Maria **shuddered** with fear when she saw the snake.*

tremble
*We felt the ground **tremble** as the giant came near.*

vibrate
*When our old car was running, everything on it used to **vibrate**.*

wobble
*"Don't let the jelly **wobble** too much," warned Mum.*

shake (2) VERB

If you **shake** something, it moves from side to side or up and down.

agitate
***Agitate** the liquid until it becomes cloudy.*

brandish
*The knight galloped towards his foe, **brandishing** a sword over his head.*

flourish
*Mehmet **flourished** his letter. "I've won!" he shouted.*

waggle
*She **waggled** her fingers at the baby to make him laugh.*

wave
*Passengers **wave** handkerchiefs when their ship sails away.*

shake (3) VERB

If something **shakes** you, it shocks and upsets you.

distress
*The bad news was bound to **distress** her.*

disturb
*The noise of the fireworks **disturbed** the animals.*

rattle
*Abel was staring into space. Something had obviously **rattled** him.*

shock
*The accident **shocked** Grandpa.*

unnerve
*The size of the rock he was expected to climb **unnerved** Calum.*

upset
*The phone call **upset** Chloe.*

shape

shape (1) NOUN

The **shape** of something is the form of its outline.

figure
*The **figure** of a man emerged from the morning mist.*

form
*Suddenly the witch took on the **form** of a toad.*

outline
*In the poor light they could see only the **outline** of an animal.*

shape (2) NOUN

A **shape** is something that has its outside edges joining in a particular way. Shapes can be flat, like a circle or triangle, or solid, like a cube or sphere.

FLAT SHAPES:

circle	oblong	rectangle
diamond	octagon	semicircle
heptagon	oval	square
hexagon	pentagon	star
kite	quadrilateral	triangle

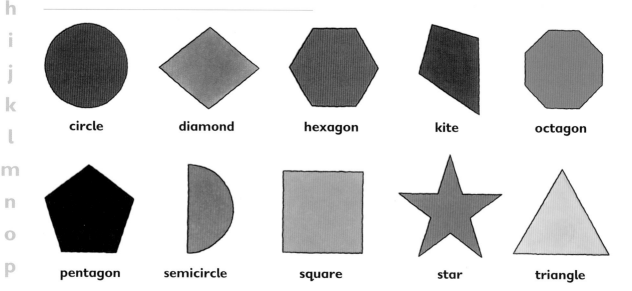

circle   diamond   hexagon   kite   octagon

pentagon   semicircle   square   star   triangle

SOLID SHAPES:

cone	hemisphere
cube	pyramid
cuboid	sphere
cylinder	

cone   cube   cuboid

cylinder   hemisphere   pyramids   sphere

a b c d e f g h i j k l m n o p q r Ss t u v w x y z

share VERB

If you **share** something among a group of people, you divide it so that everyone gets some.

divide
They divided the chocolate cake into eight equal pieces.

split
Our school decided to split the money between two charities.

sharp (1) ADJECTIVE

A **sharp** object has a fine edge or point that is good for cutting or piercing things.

jagged
Roderick cut himself on a jagged piece of glass.

keen
Be careful with that knife. It has a very keen blade.

pointed
Marianne used a pointed stick to write a message in the sand.

ANTONYM: blunt

sharp (2) ADJECTIVE

A **sharp** person is quick to notice or understand things.

bright
Only bright people can go on this television quiz show.

clever
A clever vet instantly knew what was wrong with our hamster.

observant
The baby is really observant. She noticed my earrings.

quick
Duncan is quick. You only have to tell him something once.

quick-witted
Samuel was quick-witted enough to foil the burglar.

shelter NOUN

A **shelter** is a small building or covered place where people or animals can be safe from bad weather or danger.

cover
When it started to pour, they ran for cover.

protection
The stable gave the horse protection from bad weather.

refuge
They took refuge from the storm in an old barn.

safety
Just in time, the rabbit dived for the safety of its burrow.

screen
A high wall provided a screen for tender young plants.

shine VERB

If something **shines**, it gives out a bright light.

flash
A lantern flashed in the window of the broken-down old house.

flicker
Rosita's candle flickered as she climbed the stairs.

glimmer
Lanterns glimmered in the garden.

glow
The magic stone glowed in the half-light of the cave.

twinkle
It was a fine night, and stars twinkled in the sky.

short (1) ADJECTIVE

Someone or something **short** is small in height.

little
*On the corner of the house was a **little** tower.*

low
*There was a **low** fence around the children's play area.*

small
*Becky was **small** for her age, so she played younger parts in the drama group.*

tiny
*The elf was so **tiny** he could comfortably sit on a mushroom.*

ANTONYM: tall

short (2) ADJECTIVE

A **short** period of time does not last very long.

brief
*The head teacher gave a **brief** talk before lessons began.*

fleeting
*"We've only got time for a **fleeting** visit," said Whitney.*

momentary
*There was a **momentary** pause before he spoke again.*

quick
*"We could take a **quick** break now, if you're tired," he said.*

shout VERB

If you **shout** something, you say it very loudly.

bellow
*"What are you doing in my field?" **bellowed** the farmer.*

call
*Michelle twisted her ankle and had to **call** for help.*

cry
*"Let me do it!" she **cried**.*

roar
*"I know you!" he **roared**. "You're the ones who broke my window."*

scream
*They **screamed** with terror when they saw the ghost.*

yell
*"You don't have to **yell** like that," said Mum. "I can hear you perfectly well."*

show (1) VERB

If you **show** someone how to do something, you do it yourself so that they can watch you.

demonstrate
*The teacher **demonstrated** how to use a camera.*

explain
*Grandma asked me to **explain** how the computer worked.*

teach
*Christopher **taught** his little sister how to draw horses.*

show (2) VERB

If you **show** someone something, you let them see it.

display
Sean **displayed** his project with the others.

exhibit
At the end of term the children **exhibited** their paintings.

reveal
The captured spy was unwilling to **reveal** his true identity.

show (3) NOUN

A **show** is something that you watch, sometimes at the theatre or on television.

display
There was a huge **display** of fireworks on bonfire night.

exhibition
The local art club is having an **exhibition** next week.

performance
Emma had never been on television before and was nervous about the **performance**.

show (4) VERB

If you **show** that something is true, you prove it.

confirm
"Can you **confirm** you were at home last night?" asked the police officer.

demonstrate
Julian **demonstrated** his honesty by handing in the money he had found.

prove
Rosie **proved** she could look after a pet.

shrill ADJECTIVE

A **shrill** sound is loud and high-pitched, like a whistle.

high-pitched
The sound was so **high-pitched** he had to clap his hands over his ears.

piercing
Johnny let out a **piercing** cry when the animal bit him.

screeching
The children knew that there was an owl outside. It kept them awake with its **screeching** call.

sharp
The signal was to be a **sharp** blast on the captain's whistle.

→ ear-piercing; ear-splitting

shut VERB

If you **shut** something such as a door, you move it so that it fills a gap.

close
They were asked to **close** gates after them, to stop animals straying.

fasten
The queen checked her jewels and **fastened** the box.

lock
We **locked** the door of the hutch to keep the rabbit safe.

slam
We could tell Alexandra was cross again. There was a loud bang as she **slammed** the kitchen door.

ANTONYM: open

a
b
c
d
e
f
g
h
i
j
k
l
m
n
o
p
q
r
Ss
t
u
v
w
x
y
z

shy

shy ADJECTIVE

A **shy** person or animal is nervous with people they do not know well.

cautious
Our cat is **cautious** with strangers.

modest
She's very **modest** and doesn't like to talk about her achievements.

nervous
I feel a bit **nervous** when I have to read things out in class.

timid
Her brother looks tough, but he's as **timid** as a mouse.

wary
Andrew's new dog is **wary** of anyone it doesn't know.

ANTONYM: bold

silent ADJECTIVE

If someone or something is **silent**, they do not say anything or make any noise.

dumb
They were all **dumb** with amazement at the sight of the castle.

quiet
It was unusually **quiet** in the wood now everything was covered in snow.

soundless
Her footsteps were **soundless** as she moved swiftly across the floor.

wordless
Peter watched the dancers' performance in **wordless** admiration.

silly ADJECTIVE

If someone says you are **silly**, they mean you are behaving in a foolish or childish way.

daft
I don't know where you get your **daft** ideas.

foolish
"That was a **foolish** thing to do," said the class teacher.

idiotic
He wanted us to play some **idiotic** game.

ridiculous
Some people came on the trek wearing **ridiculous** shoes.

stupid
I was **stupid** enough to listen to him.

skip VERB

When you **skip**, you step forward and hop, first with one foot and then the other.

bounce
She jumped up in delight and **bounced** over to greet him.

caper
The jester made jokes and **capered** before the king.

dance
To their amazement, a fairy **danced** lightly across the grass in front of them.

hop
She **hopped** over the rope as they spun it faster and faster.

leap
He tried to catch her, but she **leaped** away, laughing wildly.

sleep VERB

When you **sleep**, you close your eyes and your whole body rests.

doze
The cat dozed in an armchair.

drop off INFORMAL
The party next door was so loud that Nora found it hard to drop off.

hibernate
Animals that are going to hibernate in winter have to build up their fat.

nod off INFORMAL
This is important. I don't want to see anyone nodding off.

take a nap
The baby has to take a nap after lunch or he'll cry all afternoon.

slide VERB

When something **slides**, it moves smoothly over a surface.

glide
The ghost glided over the frosty ground towards them.

skate
One car skated across the road on a patch of ice.

skid
Matthew skidded to a halt, narrowly missing the head teacher.

slip
Esther slipped in the mud and crashed to the ground.

slither
A snake slithered across their path and disappeared into the bushes.

slippery ADJECTIVE

Something that is **slippery** is smooth, wet or greasy. It is difficult to keep hold of or to walk on.

greasy
The door handle was so greasy he couldn't turn it.

icy
Mind how you walk on the pavement as it's very icy.

oily
Uncle Manfred's car skidded on an oily patch in the road.

slimy
Mark tried to hold the soap but it was too wet and slimy.

slow ADJECTIVE

Something that is **slow** moves along without much speed.

dawdling
Jitendra dashed past a dawdling crowd of nursery children.

sluggish
Carol's computer was old and rather sluggish and she wanted a new one.

straggling
The guide was trying to hurry a straggling group of tourists.

unhurried
Three-toed sloths made their unhurried way through the jungle.

sly ADJECTIVE

Someone who is **sly** is good at tricking people in a not very nice way.

crafty
You have to watch him because he's a crafty little boy.

cunning
She seems charming, but actually she can be quite cunning.

devious
They are devious when it comes to getting their own way.

small

small ADJECTIVE
Something that is **small** is not as large as other things of the same kind.

little
Alice could not get through the **little** door into the garden.

minute
The wizard brushed a **minute** crumb from his cloak.

narrow
Nathan squeezed through a **narrow** opening in the fence.

tiny
The doll's house was full of **tiny** furniture.

ANTONYM: large

smart (1) ADJECTIVE
Someone who is **smart** looks neat and clean.

elegant
The film star looked **elegant** in his designer dinner suit.

neat
James wore a **neat** jacket instead of his usual jumper.

well-dressed
When he was off-stage, the clown was always **well-dressed**.

ANTONYM: scruffy

smart (2) ADJECTIVE
Smart can mean clever and intelligent.

bright
Charlotte was by far the **brightest** child in her class.

clever
Our dog can do lots of **clever** tricks.

intelligent
Let's see if anyone's **intelligent** enough to solve the problem.

sharp
Dad thought the man was a bit too **sharp**.

smell (1) NOUN
A **smell** is what you can sense through your nose.

aroma
They breathed in the delicious **aroma** of new bread.

fragrance
Adele always chose roses for their lovely light **fragrance**.

odour
There was an unpleasant **odour** coming from the cave.

scent
Harold caught the **scent** of supper.

stink
At the dump, the **stink** of rotting vegetables was overpowering.

smell (2) VERB
If something **smells**, people's noses tell them it is unpleasant.

pong INFORMAL
"Your trainers **pong** a bit," said Grandad. "Leave them outside."

reek
The room **reeked** of cigarette smoke so we opened the windows.

stink
The chemistry lab **stank** for several days after the explosion.

→ stink to high heaven

smile VERB

When you **smile**, the corners of your mouth move upwards, and you look happy.

beam
*The baby **beamed** when he saw his mum.*

grin
*Alice saw the Cheshire cat **grinning** at her.*

smirk
*Lauren **smirked** at the boys. "That's where you're wrong," she said.*

smooth ADJECTIVE

If something is **smooth**, it is not rough or bumpy.

silky
*Holly stroked the kitten's **silky** fur.*

sleek
*Michiko envied her sister's **sleek** hair.*

soft
*The baby's skin was incredibly **soft**.*

velvety
*Moles have dark, **velvety** coats.*

ANTONYM: rough

snatch VERB

If you **snatch** something, you take it quickly and suddenly.

grab
*The boy **grabbed** an apple from the cart as he ran past.*

grasp
*The prince suddenly **grasped** her hand. "Please help me," he said.*

seize
*Robin Hood **seized** a stick and fought the Sheriff of Nottingham's men.*

soft (1) ADJECTIVE

Something that is **soft** changes shape easily when you touch it.

downy
*The owl had white **downy** feathers.*

fluffy
*Ducklings' feathers are very **fluffy**.*

silky
*The unicorn had a long, **silky** mane.*

squashy
*All those tomatoes we grew are getting a bit **squashy**.*

ANTONYM: hard

soft (2) ADJECTIVE

A **soft** sound or voice is quiet and gentle.

gentle
*My great-grandfather always speaks in **gentle** tones.*

low
*The fairy's voice was so **low** they could hardly hear it.*

quiet
*Rosaleen sang the baby to sleep with a **quiet** lullaby.*

soft (3) ADJECTIVE

A **soft** light or colour is not too bright.

dim
*In the baby's room, a **dim** light stays on all night.*

faint
*A **faint** rectangle of light at the window showed it was morning.*

pale
*Hannah chose a **pale** yellow colour for her bedroom walls.*

ANTONYM: bright

a b c d e f g h i j k l m n o p q r **Ss** t u v w x y z

solve

solve VERB

If you **solve** a problem, you find an answer to it.

clear up

We've got one more thing to **clear up**. Who let the cat out?

crack

It was a hard case to **crack**. The police had been working on it for weeks.

explain

"Well, that **explains** the mystery of the strange footprint," said the inspector.

get to the bottom of

Mum never **got to the bottom of** the question of the missing doughnut.

resolve

The matter was finally **resolved** when they caught the thief red-handed.

unravel

It was a fascinating puzzle and we enjoyed **unravelling** it.

work out

They tried all morning, but couldn't **work out** the riddle.

song NOUN

A **song** is a piece of music with words.

KINDS OF SONGS:

anthem	lullaby
ballad	nursery rhyme
carol	pop song
chant	rap
folk song	round
hymn	

sorry (1) ADJECTIVE

If you feel **sorry** about something, you wish you had not done it.

apologetic

Tony was **apologetic** when he broke the kitchen window.

regretful

She was **regretful** about the problems she had caused.

sorry (2) ADJECTIVE

If you feel **sorry** for someone, you feel sad for them.

full of pity

He felt **full of pity** for the sick animals at the surgery.

sad

It made Vicky **sad** to read about children without shoes.

sympathetic

Spencer felt **sympathetic** when the goalkeeper let a ball through.

sort (1) NOUN

The different **sorts** of something are the different kinds of it.

brand

Which **brand** of cereal do you have for your breakfast?

breed

A terrier is a **breed** of dog.

kind

What **kind** of animal is that?

variety

I love all **varieties** of sweets.

sort (2) VERB

If you **sort** things, you put them into groups.

arrange

Christina **arranged** all her books into alphabetical order.

grade

The eggs were **graded** according to size.

group

Children with the same interests were **grouped** into pairs.

organize

The teacher quickly **organized** them into four teams.

sound NOUN

A **sound** is something that you hear.

ANIMAL SOUNDS:

dogs:
bark   whimper
growl   whine
snarl   yap

cats:
howl   purr
mew   spit
miaow

insects:
buzz   murmur
hum   whine

horses:
neigh
snort
whinny

OTHER ANIMAL SOUNDS:
a bull bellows
a cow lows or moos
a donkey brays
an elephant trumpets
a frog croaks
a kookaburra laughs
a lion roars or purrs

a monkey chatters
a mouse squeaks
an owl hoots or screeches
a pig grunts or snuffles
a seagull mews or screams
a sheep bleats

SOUNDS IN AN OLD HOUSE:
doors groaning
floorboards creaking
mice skittering
shutters banging
wind howling
windows rattling

WATER SOUNDS:
a brook gurgling
a fountain playing
rain pattering or splashing
a river raging
a spring bubbling
a tap dripping
a waterfall thundering

WOODLAND SOUNDS:
birdsong
branches creaking
harsh bird cries
leaves rustling
old trees groaning
small animals scuffling
twigs cracking
wind sighing
woodpecker tapping

space

space (1) NOUN

Space is the area that is empty in a place, building or container.

capacity

*The theatre had the **capacity** to seat a thousand people.*

room

*There was plenty of **room** round the table for the whole family.*

space (2) NOUN

A **space** is a gap between two things.

distance

*Measure the **distance** between the tables.*

gap

*There was a **gap** where Andrew had lost a tooth.*

space (3) NOUN

Space is the place far above the Earth where there is no air.

MANUFACTURED OBJECTS IN SPACE:

rockets	space probes
satellites	space stations
spacecraft	space telescopes

rocket

satellite

space station

NATURAL OBJECTS IN SPACE:

asteroids	planets
comets	stars
meteoroids	suns
moons	

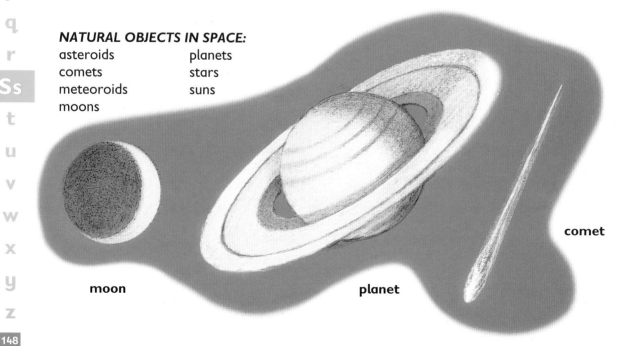

comet

moon

planet

sparkle VERB

If something **sparkles**, it shines with a lot of small bright points of light.

dance
Julia's eyes danced with mischief.

glint
When they opened the treasure chest, jewels glinted in the light.

glisten
The sea was calm, glistening in the rays of the sun.

glitter
A diamond ring glittered on the princess's right hand.

shimmer
Her dress shimmered with hundreds of tiny sequins.

twinkle
Stars twinkled in the cloudless sky.

special (1) ADJECTIVE

Something that is **special** is more important or better than other things of its kind.

extraordinary
David had an extraordinary gift for imitating animals.

important
"This is an important day for everyone," said the head teacher.

unusual
Today there was an unusual feeling of excitement in the class.

→ out of the ordinary

special (2) ADJECTIVE

Special can also mean that something is for a particular use.

particular
The job they were doing needed a particular tool.

specific
An optician carried out a specific test to check Ryan's eyesight.

spill VERB

If you **spill** something such as a liquid, you let it flow out of a container by mistake.

scatter
Matt dropped the bucket and scattered seed everywhere.

slop
Careful! You're slopping milk all over the clean tablecloth.

tip
The baby picked up his plate and tipped cereal down his jumper.

upset
Alison waved an arm and upset the jug of fruit juice.

spin VERB

When somebody or something **spins**, they turn round quickly.

revolve
A sprinkler was revolving in the middle of the lawn, watering the grass.

rotate
Blades began to rotate and the helicopter roared off into the sky.

turn
When he gets angry he turns on his heel and stalks off.

whirl
In this scene, the ballerina whirls faster and faster until she becomes a white blur on the stage.

sport

sport NOUN

Sports are games you play that exercise your body.

DIFFERENT SPORTS:

baseball	skating
basketball	skiing
boxing	snooker
cricket	soccer
darts	squash
fishing	surfing
football	swimming
hockey	table tennis
netball	tennis
rugby	volleyball
running	wrestling
sailing	

basketball

surfing

sailing

skiing

snooker

spot (1) NOUN

A **spot** is a small round mark on a surface.

blot
*His new fountain pen scattered **blots** all over the page.*

dot
*The doll was wearing a white dress with pink **dots**.*

mark
*No matter how hard he tried, he couldn't get rid of the black **mark** on his shirt.*

smudge
*You've got a **smudge** of green paint on your forehead.*

speck
*She was fussy about even the tiniest **speck** of dirt on her clothes.*

spot (2) NOUN

A **spot** can be a particular place.

location
*Our holiday cottage is in a beautiful **location** by a lake.*

place
*We need to find a good shady **place** for the picnic.*

point
*They left a small mound of stones to mark the **point** where they turned right.*

position
*They dragged their bikes to a **position** where they would not be seen.*

site
*Burned grass marked the **site** where someone had camped recently.*

spot (3) VERB

If you **spot** something, you notice it.

catch sight of
*Suddenly, they **caught sight of** a tiny man dressed in green.*

detect
*She **detected** a slight movement in the murky water.*

make out
*We **made out** a dark shape in the mist.*

see
*Let me know if you **see** anybody.*

spread VERB

If you **spread** something, you arrange it over a surface.

arrange
*They **arranged** their wet clothes on the grass to dry in the sun.*

lay out
*Chrissie proudly **laid out** her artwork on the table.*

squeeze VERB

If you **squeeze** something into a small space, you manage to fit it in.

cram
*She **crammed** the whole slice of cake into her mouth.*

crowd
*People **crowded** into the tiny room.*

jam
*He **jammed** two more books into his bag.*

pack
*"I'm sorry," said the bus driver. "I can't **pack** any more in."*

squirt VERB

If a liquid **squirts**, it comes out of a narrow opening in a thin fast stream.

shoot
Jeremy turned the hose on his brother and **shot** water all over him.

spout
The fountain in the park **spouts** water ten metres in the air.

spurt
Diesel **spurted** from the fuel tank and the lorry had to stop.

squeeze
Angelica **squeezed** lemon juice into the cake mixture.

stream
Dad hit a pipe with a nail and water **streamed** out.

stand (1) VERB

When you **stand**, you get to your feet and your body is upright.

get up
He **got up** to give an old lady his seat on the bus.

rise
Everyone **rose** when the judge entered the law court.

stand (2) VERB

If you **stand** something somewhere, you put it there in an upright position.

arrange
Could you please **arrange** the dried flowers in that tall jug?

erect
The brothers **erected** the tent in the middle of the lawn.

place
Mrs Jones carefully **placed** a vase on the hall table.

position
Wherever she **positioned** the china figure it somehow looked odd.

start (1) VERB

To **start** means to begin.

begin
Reginald took up a pen and **began** to write his letter.

commence
"When you are quiet," snarled the professor, "I will **commence** my lecture."

proceed
Tim gave a small cough to get everyone's attention. Then he **proceeded** to read his poem.

→ get under way

ANTONYM: finish

start (2) VERB

When someone **starts** something new, they create it or cause it to begin.

create
The teenagers wanted to **create** a youth club in the village.

establish
Local parents were trying to **establish** a child-minding service to take care of children after school.

introduce
The teacher said she would **introduce** a new system next term.

launch
The department store has **launched** a new range of toys.

set up
My sister wants to **set up** a fan club for her favourite band.

state VERB

If you **state** something, you say it clearly and formally.

announce
Hugh **announced** he intended to be a champion tennis player one day.

assert
Rachel **asserted** it was her right to be in charge of the garden project.

declare
Sophie **declared** she would never speak to her friend again.

say
"It's my turn," **said** Indigo, "and that's all there is to it."

stay VERB

If you **stay** in a place, you do not move away from it.

hang around INFORMAL
"I'm not going to **hang around** here a moment longer," said Sebastian crossly. "I'm going home."

linger
Children **lingered** in the playground waiting for the coach to arrive.

loiter
"You mustn't **loiter** here," said the police officer firmly.

remain
They had to **remain** at school till their dad could fetch them.

wait
"**Wait** there," said Jake. "I'll just go and have a look."

stop (1) VERB

If you **stop** what you are doing, you no longer do it.

conclude
"I will **conclude**," said the Mayor, "with a vote of thanks."

end
The carousel ride **ended** after two minutes.

finish
Clare **finished** reading her book and went to bed.

give up
Dad decided to **give up** eating chocolate for a month.

quit
Emmanuel wanted to **quit** football and take up basketball instead.

stop (2) VERB

To **stop** can mean to prevent something.

ban
We were **banned** from watching TV until we'd done our homework.

block
Traffic on the motorway was **blocked** by a bad accident.

hold back
A dam **held back** the water.

interrupt
The teacher **interrupted** a scuffle at the back of the class.

→ nip something in the bud

story NOUN

A **story** tells you about things that have happened. It can be about something real or something made up.

account
*The teacher asked them to write an **account** of their visit to the castle.*

anecdote
*My uncle is full of **anecdotes** about his life in the army.*

narrative
*The knight told a **narrative** of his battle with the foe.*

tale
*Nicholas liked to read **tales** about magic and mystery.*

KINDS OF STORIES:

fiction

adventure	legend
comedy	myth
crime	parable
fable	romance
fairy tale	science fiction
fantasy	thriller
ghost story	

fairy tale

non-fiction

autobiography	instructions
biography	recipe
explanation	report

strain (1) VERB

If you **strain** to do something, you try too hard.

struggle
*The boys **struggled** to shift the rock, but it was hopeless.*

try hard
*He **tried hard** to move the old wardrobe out of the bedroom.*

wrench
*They **wrenched** with all their might, but the door refused to open.*

strain (2) VERB

If you **strain** something like a muscle, you injure it by moving awkwardly.

damage
*He **damaged** a tendon when he twisted his foot.*

hurt
*"You'll **hurt** yourself if you try to lift that," said his mum.*

injure
*The footballer **injured** a calf muscle and had to leave the field.*

strange (1) ADJECTIVE

Something that is **strange** is odd or unexpected.

curious
*Alice thought it **curious** that the White Rabbit had a watch.*

exceptional
*It was **exceptional** weather for that time of year.*

extraordinary

*The spider was **extraordinary**. She'd never seen one like it before.*

funny

*Our car was making a **funny** noise, then steam came out of the engine.*

odd

*"That's **odd**," said Ellie. "I'm sure that tree wasn't there yesterday."*

peculiar

*A **peculiar** burning smell came from the witch's cauldron.*

remarkable

*They found some **remarkable** footprints in the snow.*

weird

*The children found a map with **weird** writing all over it.*

→ bizarre; mystifying

strange (2) ADJECTIVE

A **strange** place is one you have never been to before.

foreign

*He was not far from home, but the area seemed **foreign**.*

new

*While she was on holiday, Kim was happy to explore **new** towns.*

unfamiliar

*Abdullah's dog was always anxious in **unfamiliar** places.*

ANTONYM: familiar

stray VERB

If people or animals **stray**, they wander away.

be lost

*Our cat **was lost** for a week when we moved house.*

go astray

*Someone left the gate open and all the sheep **went astray**.*

straggle

*A few of the children **straggled** out into the garden.*

wander

*Samantha didn't notice she had **wandered** away from her brothers.*

strict ADJECTIVE

Someone or something **strict** must be obeyed.

firm

*The drama teacher is always very **firm** at rehearsals.*

rigid

*Victorian fathers were often **rigid** in dealing with their families.*

rigorous

*We have to follow **rigorous** rules when we are doing research.*

severe

*There were notices everywhere with **severe** warnings about trespassing.*

stern

*Our hearts sank when we saw the **stern** expression on Gran's face.*

strong

strong (1) ADJECTIVE

If you are **strong**, you can work hard and carry heavy things.

brawny
A **brawny** man carried their cases up four flights of stairs.

hefty
It took two **hefty** firemen to hold the hose that put out the fire.

mighty
With one **mighty** blow, the knight slew the huge dragon.

powerful
The woodcutter took hold of the axe in a **powerful** grip.

tough
Wrestlers have to be very **tough**.

ANTONYM: weak

strong (2) ADJECTIVE

Objects or materials that are **strong** will last well.

hard-wearing
The walkers' boots and jackets were made of **hard-wearing** material.

heavy-duty
The school has **heavy-duty** flooring in the sports hall.

sturdy
Robbie swung up on to a **sturdy** branch.

well-built
The castle had to be **well-built** to withstand the pounding waves.

strong (3) ADJECTIVE

Strong can mean deeply felt.

deep
There was a **deep** friendship between them.

fierce
Peter's friends knew they could count on his **fierce** loyalty.

keen
Jessie had a **keen** interest in all sports.

struggle VERB

If you **struggle** to do something, you try hard to do it but find it difficult.

exert yourself
Sayyid had to **exert himself** to be nice to his cousin.

make every effort
Lois **made every effort** to get in the team, but it didn't work.

strain
They **strained** to lift the sack, but it was too heavy.

work hard
The whole class **worked hard** with the history project.

→ work like a Trojan

stubborn ADJECTIVE

Someone who is **stubborn** is determined to do what they want.

defiant
Toby was in a **defiant** mood and refused to help clean the car.

difficult
Emerenzia can be **difficult** if you don't ask her nicely.

dogged
He won a place in the team through his **dogged** determination.

inflexible
Natalie is **inflexible** in her aim to become a famous writer.

obstinate
Her mouth was set in an **obstinate** line.

pig-headed
*Oliver was usually too **pig-headed** to listen to anybody.*

wilful
*My sister is so **wilful** that she's always getting into trouble.*

study (1) VERB
*If you **study** a subject, you spend time learning about it.*

learn
*Alex went to France for the summer to **learn** the language.*

read up on
*Holly had been **reading up on** how to look after guinea pigs.*

swot INFORMAL
*Matt said he was going to have to **swot** for his exams.*

study (2) VERB
*If you **study** something, you look at it carefully.*

examine
*Kimberly **examined** her new science book with interest.*

investigate
*Sherlock Holmes liked to **investigate** unusual cases.*

look into
*The head teacher said she would **look into** the problem.*

research
*Scientists are always **researching** diseases and trying to find cures.*

stuffy ADJECTIVE
If a place is **stuffy**, there is not enough fresh air in it.

close
*They could hardly breathe because the air was so **close**.*

heavy
*The air was **heavy** with smoke, so the children stayed inside.*

muggy
*The **muggy** day made them all feel limp and listless.*

stale
*The air in the dragon's cave was **stale** and smelled of burning toast.*

stifling
*Great-grandma's room is always **stifling**, but that's how she likes it.*

warm
*It was so **warm** we had to fling open all the windows.*

stupid ADJECTIVE
Stupid people or ideas are not at all bright or sensible.

dim INFORMAL
*The book was so hard to read it made me feel **dim**.*

foolish
*Debbie suddenly realized it would be a **foolish** thing to do.*

half-baked
*Don't listen to his **half-baked** ideas.*

idiotic
*It's **idiotic** to go out in a boat without a life jacket.*

a b c d e f g h i j k l m n o p q r **Ss** t u v w x y z

sudden ADJECTIVE

Something that is **sudden** happens quickly and unexpectedly.

abrupt

*There was an **abrupt** change in his manner when we told him the truth.*

hasty

*Alex made a **hasty** exit when he saw his father's expression.*

hurried

*Jack's departure was **hurried**. He had spotted a giant coming towards him.*

quick

*After a moment, she gave a **quick** smile. "That's fine," she said.*

rash

*It was a **rash** decision but luckily things turned out well.*

swift

*With a **swift** movement, the magician produced an egg from Tony's ear.*

unexpected

*The prince's invitation was **unexpected**, and the lady had nothing to wear.*

support (1) VERB

If you **support** someone, you want to help them.

back

*At school, everyone **backs** their own team.*

defend

*Sarah was always ready to **defend** her friends at school.*

encourage

*The drama teacher **encouraged** Katie with her acting.*

help

*Ian's parents **helped** him a lot.*

side with

*In any argument, Shane always **sided with** his brother.*

stand up for

*Steven was quite young when he learned to **stand up for** himself.*

support (2) VERB

If something **supports** an object, it holds it up firmly.

brace

*Emily **braced** herself against the table.*

hold up

*The old lady used a forked stick to **hold up** her washing line.*

prop up

*Dad used lots of poles to **prop up** the tent.*

reinforce

*Builders **reinforced** the fence with a few concrete posts.*

sure (1) ADJECTIVE

If you are **sure** something is true, you believe it is true.

certain

*Kylie was **certain** she'd brought her work home, but it wasn't there.*

confident

*The team was **confident** it would win the game.*

convinced

*Both boys were **convinced** someone was following them.*

positive

*"Are you **positive** you gave me back that book?" she asked.*

satisfied

*The teacher was **satisfied** that they were telling the truth.*

a b c d e f g h i j k l m n o p q r **Ss** t u v w x y z

sure (2) ADJECTIVE

You say something is **sure** when it can be relied on.

effective
*Grandma knew all sorts of **effective** remedies for my cold.*

reliable
*Looking for droppings is a **reliable** way of tracking animals.*

surprise (1) NOUN

A **surprise** is something unexpected.

bombshell
*The loss of their best goalkeeper came as a **bombshell**.*

shock
*The news that her friend was leaving was a **shock** to Rosie.*

→ bolt from the blue

surprise (2) NOUN

Surprise can be the way you feel about something unexpected.

amazement
*Libby stared at the tiny orange fellow in **amazement**. "What on earth are you?" she whispered.*

astonishment
*Shani watched in **astonishment** when she saw herself on television.*

wonder
*They gazed in **wonder** at the spectacular scene before them.*

surprise (3) VERB

If something **surprises** you, it gives you a feeling of surprise.

amaze
*The wonderful treasures Aladdin found **amazed** and delighted him.*

astonish
*The skill of the ice skaters **astonished** her.*

stagger
*The sight of the feast spread on the table **staggered** him.*

startle
*The coldness of the sea water **startled** Laura.*

stun
*Benjamin **stunned** the audience with his dance performance.*

swell VERB

If something **swells**, it becomes larger and rounder than usual.

bloat
*He ate so much birthday cake his stomach **bloated** uncomfortably.*

bulge
*The ogre's belly **bulged** over his belt.*

get bigger
*Mr Jones measured the pumpkins every day, willing them to **get bigger**.*

grow
*Before his horrified eyes, the toad **grew** to an enormous size.*

a b c d e f g h i j k l m n o p q r **Ss** t u v w x y z

Tt

take (1) VERB

If you **take** something, you put your hand round it and carry it.

carry
*Let me **carry** your books for you.*

clasp
*Katherine **clasped** the baby in her arms.*

grip
*"**Grip** the handle with both hands. This bag is heavy," said my cousin.*

hold
*He offered to **hold** her coat while she looked in her bag.*

take (2) VERB

If someone **takes** you somewhere, you go there with them.

bring
*You can **bring** a friend to the party if you want to.*

guide
*"I'll **guide** you on the first part of the journey," said the wizard.*

lead
*Spot **led** Julia to his favourite park.*

take (3) VERB

If a person **takes** something that does not belong to them, they steal it.

grab
*Alexander **grabbed** an apple from his neighbour's tree.*

snatch
*The thief **snatched** a diamond ring and ran from the shop.*

steal
*Thomas saw an old man **steal** a book and slip out of the back door.*

talent NOUN

Talent is the natural ability a person has to do something well.

ability
*Charlotte was featured on TV because of her musical **ability**.*

aptitude
*Kerena has an **aptitude** for working with little children.*

flair
*Jeremy showed a **flair** for drawing when he was very young.*

genius
*Ms Kent's **genius** as a teacher makes her lessons exciting.*

gift
*My grandad has a **gift** for making people feel confident.*

knack
*"It takes a special **knack** to build these model kits," Simon said.*

skill
*The children admired the conjuror's **skill**.*

talk (1) VERB

When you **talk**, you say things to someone.

chat
*My sister can **chat** on the phone for hours.*

converse
*We are learning to **converse** in French.*

gossip
*Old men would stand **gossiping** on the corner all day.*

prattle
*Tom couldn't stop **prattling** about his summer holiday.*

speak
*Tony had plenty to say, but they wouldn't let him **speak**.*

talk (2) NOUN

A **talk** is an informal speech.

address
*The head teacher gave a short **address** welcoming the parents.*

lecture
*The professor's **lecture** was about endangered wild animals.*

report
*Robert gave a detailed **report** on the football match.*

sermon
*The vicar's **sermon** was a bit long.*

speech
*There was a **speech** before the prizes were given out.*

tall ADJECTIVE

Something **tall** is higher than average.

giant
*A **giant** statue stood in the park.*

high
*Charles lived on the top floor of a **high** block of flats.*

lanky
*A **lanky** young man played music for them on his guitar.*

soaring
*They gazed up from the beach at **soaring** white cliffs.*

towering
*Joe found himself in a sunny clearing surrounded by **towering** trees.*

ANTONYM: short

tame ADJECTIVE

A **tame** animal is not afraid of humans and will not hurt them.

docile
*Some pet parrots can be a bit vicious, but Sam's is really **docile**.*

domesticated
***Domesticated** animals help humans in lots of ways.*

gentle
*Most pets are **gentle** and easy to handle.*

obedient
*However **obedient** that elephant seems, it's still dangerous.*

ANTONYM: wild

a b c d e f g h i j k l m n o p q r s **Tt** u v w x y z

taste

taste (1) NOUN

The **taste** of something is the flavour of it.

flavour
*I love the **flavour** of strawberry jam.*

tang
*The sharp **tang** of lemon is refreshing.*

taste (2) NOUN

If you have a **taste** of food or drink, you try a small amount of it.

bit
*I'll try a little **bit**, but I don't think I'll like it.*

bite
*"Can I have a **bite** of your burger too?" asked Dee, as she reached for a chip.*

drop
*George pestered Grandpa for a **drop** of his hot tea.*

morsel
*Mum gave the baby a **morsel** of egg to see if he would eat it.*

mouthful
*One **mouthful** of the soup was enough.*

nibble
*Jeremy handed him a broken piece of biscuit. "There's only a **nibble** left," he said.*

sip
*"Just a **sip**," she pleaded.*

spoonful
*The cook had a **spoonful** of the stew, and smiled. "That's fine," she said.*

tear VERB

If you **tear** something, such as paper or fabric, you pull it apart.

claw
*"Don't let the kitten **claw** a hole in your new jumper," said Auntie.*

divide
***Divide** the paper in half and give one piece to your partner.*

ladder
*Mum keeps on **laddering** her stockings on that chair.*

rip
*He didn't want to **rip** his new jeans on the barbed wire.*

scratch
*Nick didn't mean to **scratch** the wallpaper when he parked his bike in the hall.*

shred
*At the end of the story, Naomi **shreds** the letter into little pieces and bursts into tears.*

slit
*Josh was eager to **slit** open the envelope.*

split
*"The ship's sail could **split** in this weather," warned the sailor.*

tease VERB

To **tease** means to make fun of someone, or annoy them.

annoy
*Stop **annoying** your sister.*

badger
*The boys wouldn't stop **badgering** her till she agreed to go with them.*

make fun of
*It's cruel to **make fun of** people.*

pester
*If you keep **pestering** me, we won't go out at all.*

torment
*That cat will scratch you if you don't stop **tormenting** her.*

→ aggravate; needle

tell (1) VERB

If you **tell** someone something, you let them know about it.

inform
*He phoned the police to **inform** them of the burglary.*

mention
*Please don't **mention** this to anybody.*

reveal
*My friend spoilt the book by **revealing** the surprise ending.*

say
*He wouldn't **say** what he had been doing.*

warn
*It's the weather forecaster's job to **warn** us of possible flooding.*

tell (2) VERB

If someone **tells** you to do something, they say you must do it.

command
*The troops were **commanded** to move forward at dawn.*

direct
*The police officer **directed** them to leave the building immediately.*

instruct
*The pirate captain **instructed** his men to hide the treasure.*

order
*"I can't **order** you to exercise," said Dr Foster, "but it will be good for your health."*

tender ADJECTIVE

Someone who is **tender** shows gentle and caring feelings.

gentle
*My uncle's a **gentle** person who would never hurt anyone.*

kind
*Julia has a **kind** mother who comforts her when she's upset.*

loving
*Grandma gave him a **loving** kiss when they met.*

soft-hearted
*Mum is always **soft-hearted** when it comes to small animals.*

terrible ADJECTIVE

Something **terrible** is serious and unpleasant.

alarming
*An **alarming** scream ripped through the icy forest.*

appalling
*There was an **appalling** accident on the foggy motorway.*

awful
*They wrinkled their noses at the **awful** smell of burning.*

bad
*The witch made a **bad** mistake when she recited the spell.*

dreadful
***Dreadful** weather nearly ruined Natalie's birthday party.*

horrible
*A **horrible** ogre stole all the sheep.*

a b c d e f g h i j k l m n o p q r s **Tt** u v w x y z

test

test (1) VERB

If someone **tests** something, they try to find out what it is like.

check
*They **checked** the ground carefully before putting their weight on it.*

examine
*Scientists **examined** the water and declared it was pure.*

investigate
*Birdwatchers are **investigating** the way falcons hunt for food.*

research
*In class we are **researching** different ways of growing plants.*

try
*Amy **tried** the yo-yo before she decided to buy it.*

try out
*Josh **tried out** his new pen.*

test (2) NOUN

A **test** is an attempt to find out how good somebody or something is.

check
*Douglas went to the clinic for a full health **check**.*

exam
*My sister did really well in her **exam**.*

examination
*Some parts of the plane were taken away for **examination** purposes.*

trial
*Scientists were carrying out **trials** on new medication for colds.*

thick (1) ADJECTIVE

An object that is **thick** is deeper through than other things of the same kind.

deep
***Deep** layers of mud lay by the river.*

fat
*Melanie chose a nice **fat** book to read.*

solid
*A **solid** carpet of snow covered the fields.*

wide
*A **wide** privet hedge protected them from the traffic.*

ANTONYM: thin

thick (2) ADJECTIVE

Thick liquids do not flow easily.

concentrated
*The fruit juice was so **concentrated** she could stand her straw up in it.*

condensed
*Mum added water to the **condensed** soup.*

thick (3) ADJECTIVE

Thick can mean grouped closely together.

bristling
*Grandfather has a **bristling** moustache.*

dense
*The children were lost in a **dense** forest.*

luxuriant
*A maid brushed the princess's long, **luxuriant** hair.*

thin (1) ADJECTIVE

A **thin** person weighs less than most people of the same height.

bony
The wizard's old cloak hung limply on his bony shoulders.

lean
The cowboy was as lean and as tough as his horse.

scrawny
A scrawny dog came into the garden.

slender
The girl modelling the clothes was tall, dark and slender.

slim
Mum has managed to keep her slim figure.

ANTONYM: fat

thin (2) ADJECTIVE

Something that is **thin** measures a small distance from side to side.

fine
The baby's head was covered in fine hairs.

flimsy
One of the fairies wore a dress of strange, flimsy material.

light
Light curtains hung at the window.

narrow
The witch's nose was long and narrow.

sparse
A sparse beard was sprouting on his chin.

ANTONYM: thick

thin (3) ADJECTIVE

Thin liquids are weak and watery.

runny
The pancake mixture was too runny.

watery
Oliver said the soup was too watery.

weak
The jelly was too weak to set properly.

thing NOUN

A **thing** is an object, rather than an animal or a human being.

article
His case burst open and articles were scattered all over the floor.

device
They looked for a device to help them reach their kite. It was stuck high up in a tree.

item
There were lots of items on the list that they still had to pack.

object
The antique shop had several interesting objects for sale.

things PLURAL NOUN

Your **things** are your clothes or possessions.

baggage
They had to wait to collect their baggage at the airport.

belongings
The man was poor, and had very few personal belongings.

bits and pieces
Gather your bits and pieces and put them away tidily.

equipment
Dad loaded the camping equipment into the trailer.

gear
We took our swimming gear with us to the beach.

luggage
When we went on holiday, we filled our roof rack with luggage.

possessions
The film showed people with their possessions piled up in carts.

stuff
My cousin had a lot of stuff with him when he came to stay.

a
b
c
d
e
f
g
h
i
j
k
l
m
n
o
p
q
r
s
Tt
u
v
w
x
y
z

think

think (1) VERB

When you **think**, you use your mind to consider ideas or problems.

consider
You need to consider carefully what you should do.

estimate
I estimate the whole journey will take about four hours.

imagine
Ben tried to imagine how he would feel.

wonder
Do you ever wonder what it would be like to be a bird?

think (2)

If you **think** something is true, you believe it is true but you are not sure.

believe
Sam believed his parents were planning a holiday.

feel
Daisy felt she might have won a prize.

guess
We guess our teacher is going to get married soon.

reckon
"I reckon it's going to snow tonight," said Grandad.

suppose
I suppose I should get on with my work.

understand
We understand there's going to be a new doctor at the surgery.

thoughtful ADJECTIVE

A **thoughtful** person remembers what other people want or need, and tries to be kind to them.

attentive
We like that restaurant. The food is good and the staff are attentive.

caring
He's a caring boy who helps his mum.

considerate
Dad's boss is considerate. She doesn't mind him being late when he takes us all to school.

helpful
Sara took a helpful friend when she went to choose a book for her mum.

kind
"How kind of you to fetch my wand," said the wizard.

unselfish
Tom is really unselfish. He would even give you his last sweet.

throw VERB

If you **throw** an object that you are holding, you send it through the air.

fling
Joel flung his jacket on the bed.

hurl
Natalie burst into tears and hurled her book across the room.

sling
She slung her bag over one shoulder and dashed to the car.

toss
They went into the park and tossed sticks for the dog.

thrust VERB

If you **thrust** something somewhere, you push or move it there quickly with a lot of force.

force
*He **forced** the key into the lock and the door swung open.*

push
*Lara **pushed** the secret note into the pocket of her jeans.*

shove
*We **shoved** our swimming things in a bag and ran to the beach.*

tidy ADJECTIVE

Something that is **tidy** is neat and well arranged.

neat
*Everything about him is so **neat** he looks as if he never relaxes.*

orderly
*The top of her desk looks **orderly**, but the drawers are in a dreadful muddle.*

smart
*The police looked **smart** in their uniforms.*

straight
*They all worked hard and the room was **straight** in no time.*

trim
*Grandpa likes to have **trim** flowerbeds.*

uncluttered
*The house was so **uncluttered** it didn't look like a real home.*

ANTONYM: untidy

tie (1) VERB

If you **tie** an object to something, you fasten it with something like string.

bind
*They **bound** the sticks in small bundles to make them easy to carry.*

fasten
*The latch had broken, so Daniel **fastened** the gate with a piece of wire.*

knot
*The magician **knotted** scarves together, then turned them into a rabbit.*

lash
*They **lashed** planks together with rope to make a raft.*

secure
*Dad **secured** the luggage on the car before we went on holiday.*

tether
*He **tethered** the donkey to a strong post.*

tie (2) VERB

If two people or teams **tie**, they have the same score.

be level
*In the competition the two boys **were level**.*

be neck and neck
*They **were neck and neck** across the finish line and everyone cheered.*

draw
*"After an exciting game, the two teams **drew**," he said.*

time

time NOUN

Time is what is measured in seconds, minutes, hours, days and years.

MEASURING TIME:

second	
minute	60 seconds
hour	60 minutes
day	24 hours
week	7 days
fortnight	14 days
lunar month	28 days
year	365 days
leap year	366 days
decade	10 years
century	100 years
millennium	1000 years

DAYS OF THE WEEK:

Monday	Friday
Tuesday	Saturday
Wednesday	Sunday
Thursday	

NUMBER OF DAYS IN THE MONTH:

January	31
February	28 (or 29 in a leap year)
March	31
April	30
May	31
June	30
July	31
August	31
September	30
October	31
November	30
December	31

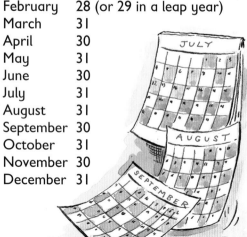

TIMES OF DAY:

dawn	noon	evening
morning	afternoon	night
midday	dusk	midnight

SEASONS:

spring	autumn
summer	winter

spring

summer

autumn

winter

HOW OFTEN:

always	sometimes
never	twice
often	usually
once	

MORE TIME WORDS:

now	tomorrow
today	yesterday

tiny ADJECTIVE

Something that is **tiny** is very small.

little

A **little** spider scuttled across Kylie's desk.

microscopic

He flicked a **microscopic** speck of dust from his jacket.

miniature

Ellie kept a **miniature** portrait of her great-grandmother on her dressing table.

minute

All I had to eat was a **minute** helping of cottage pie.

small

The shoes were **small** enough to fit a doll.

ANTONYM: huge

tip (1) NOUN

The **tip** of something long and narrow is the end of it.

end

The **end** of the cat's tail began to twitch in annoyance.

peak

Mist covered the **peak** of the mountain, so they decided not to go up.

point

Georgia likes to keep a sharp **point** on her pencils.

top

The **top** of an iceberg is always much smaller than the part below the water line.

tip (2) VERB

If you **tip** an object, you move it so that it is no longer straight.

lean

Robert **leaned** his chair back and almost lost his balance.

overturn

The boat **overturned** and they all fell into the water.

spill

Nina **spilled** her juice all over the table and chair.

tilt

If you **tilt** that jug any further you'll lose the lot.

tired ADJECTIVE

If you are **tired**, you feel that you want to rest or sleep.

exhausted

We were **exhausted** after climbing every tower in the castle.

ready to drop

By the time Patrick had walked ten miles he was **ready to drop**.

sleepy

At bedtime the baby yawned and gave her mum a **sleepy** smile.

worn out

Layla was too **worn out** to argue.

→ absolutely shattered; cream-crackered; dead on your feet

tool

tool NOUN

A **tool** is anything that you use to help you do something.

device
It's a **device** that sailors used to find their position at sea.

gadget
We need a **gadget** to hold these two bits together while they stick.

instrument
My dad has an **instrument** for measuring things really accurately.

utensil
You can't even begin this sort of cookery without a rack full of **utensils**.

top (1) NOUN

The **top** of something is its highest point, part or surface.

crest
A man on a surfboard appeared on the **crest** of a wave.

head
Rachel wrote her name and the date at the **head** of the page.

peak
Holiday firms tend to charge **peak** prices during summer.

summit
The **summit** of the mountain was covered in snow.

tip
The **tips** of the pine trees were hidden in thick mist.

top (2) NOUN

The **top** of a bottle, jar or tube is its cap or lid.

cap
Lewis poured himself a drink and put the **cap** back on the bottle.

lid
The **lid** of the jam jar rolled off the table and clattered on the floor.

touch (1) VERB

If you **touch** something, you feel it with your hand.

feel
Chloe **felt** the parcel to try to guess what was in it.

handle
Don't forget to wash your hands after you've **handled** the hamster.

pat
Jason **patted** the dog's head and stroked its soft coat.

rub
"Yum, yum!" said the ogre, **rubbing** his rounded stomach.

stroke
The cat came over to me and demanded to be **stroked**.

touch (2) VERB

If two things are **touching**, there is no space between them.

brush
His fingers accidentally **brushed** the wet paint and smudged it.

graze
"A bullet has **grazed** this soldier's arm," said the nurse.

meet
Branches **met** overhead, casting deep shadows on the road.

travel VERB

When you **travel**, you go from one place to another.

go
The family is **going** to India for a holiday this year.

make your way
Some of the hikers were planning to **make their way** up the mountain.

take a trip
Grandma wants to **take a trip** in a hot-air balloon this summer.

tree NOUN

A **tree** is a large plant with a woody trunk, branches and leaves.

KINDS OF TREES:

ash	oak
beech	palm
birch	pine
fir	poplar
holly	sycamore
horse chestnut	willow
larch	yew
maple	

maple

oak

palm

pine

willow

trick (1) NOUN

A **trick** is something that deceives someone.

con INFORMAL
*A letter claimed we could make lots of money, but it was a **con**.*

deception
*The **deception** worked and the man thought he had won a new car.*

hoax
*An ambulance rushed to the scene and discovered that the call was a stupid **hoax**.*

trick (2) VERB

If a person **tricks** someone, they deceive them.

cheat
*A wicked man **cheated** Michael's father out of some land he owned.*

con INFORMAL
*Last week someone **conned** my aunt out of her holiday savings.*

deceive
*Someone tried to **deceive** Mum by claiming he was her cousin.*

fool
*Jack **fooled** Harry into clearing up the paints in the classroom.*

trickle VERB

When a liquid **trickles**, it flows slowly in small amounts.

dribble
*Saliva sometimes **dribbles** from the baby's mouth when he's teething.*

leak
*Water was **leaking** from the kitchen tap into the sink.*

ooze
*Mud **oozed** up between her toes as she walked barefoot across the field.*

seep
*There were damp patches on the ceiling where rain was **seeping** through the roof.*

trip (1) VERB

If you **trip**, you catch your foot on something and fall over.

fall
*Darcy spun round quickly and **fell** over a paving stone.*

stumble
*The track was rough and they **stumbled** several times.*

tumble
*Kylie **tumbled** over a toy, banged her head and started to cry.*

trip (2) NOUN

A **trip** is a journey to a place and back again.

day out
*We were looking forward to a **day out** in the country.*

excursion
*The class went on an **excursion** to the Roman ruins.*

jaunt
*A large notice offered cut-price **jaunts** in a riverboat.*

journey
*It was a long **journey** and the boys were very tired.*

outing
*She wanted more books to read, so they went on an **outing** to the library.*

voyage
*Tallulah hoped the sea would be calm for the **voyage**.*

trouble (1) NOUN

Trouble is something that worries or bothers you.

bother
*Ellie had a bit of **bother** at school when she lost her glasses.*

difficulty
*They had some **difficulty** in finding the right place.*

hassle INFORMAL
*"I really don't need this **hassle** today," complained the zoo keeper.*

problem
*The **problem** was finding somewhere to practise his violin.*

trouble (2) VERB

If you **trouble** somebody, you bother them.

annoy
*Junk mail **annoys** my parents. They say it is a waste of paper.*

bother
*"Don't **bother** that cat or she'll scratch you." said Auntie Mavis.*

disturb
*It wasn't a good idea to **disturb** the wasps.*

irritate
*It **irritates** Mum if I forget to say "please" and "thank you".*

pester
*Stop **pestering** me. I'm not going to change my mind.*

worry
*Andrew was **worried** by the thought of his tree house blowing down in the storm.*

true ADJECTIVE

A **true** story or statement is based on facts and is not made up.

accurate
*They were able to give an **accurate** description of the burglar.*

correct
*This time, give me the **correct** version of the story.*

factual
*I want a **factual** report. Don't make anything up.*

genuine
*Tales of the explorer's life in the jungle are quite **genuine**.*

real
*The TV programme showed the **real** problems of being a star.*

trust VERB

If you **trust** someone, you believe that they are honest and will not do anything to hurt you.

believe
*You can always **believe** what he says.*

count on
*Can I **count on** you to back me up?*

depend on
*On an adventure like this, you need a friend you can **depend on**.*

rely on
*Now she's ill she has to **rely on** her neighbours to do the shopping.*

try

try (1) VERB

If you **try** to do something, you do your best to do it.

aim

*Andrew **aimed** to catch a big fish for supper, and he did it too!*

attempt

*Mehmet is going to **attempt** the high jump one more time.*

do your best

*Gary is not very good at woodwork, but he **does his best**.*

make an effort

*If Marcus **made an effort** he could do really well.*

struggle

*The girls **struggled** to open the door, but it was stuck fast.*

➔ have a go; have a crack; have a shot

try (2) VERB

If you **try** something, you test it to see what it is like.

check out

*Granville wanted to **check out** the new computer game.*

sample

*We decided to **sample** one of Mum's delicious fairy cakes.*

taste

*"Just **taste** it," said the chef. "You might find you like it."*

test

*The mechanic **tested** the engine and the brakes on our car.*

turn (1) NOUN

If people take **turns** to do something, they do it one after the other.

chance

*I'm sure I can do it. Just give me a **chance**.*

go

*That's not fair! It's my **go**!*

shot

*At last Mark was allowed to have a **shot**.*

try

*"Let me have a **try**," said Grandma. "I used to be good at this."*

turn (2) VERB

When someone or something **turns**, they change direction.

bend

*At the top of the hill, trees **bent** away from the wind.*

spin

*Lauren **spun** round when she heard the door open.*

swivel

*Our TV is on a bracket so that you can **swivel** it.*

twirl

*Floella **twirled** around for her mum to admire the dress.*

wind

*The hillside track **wound** back on itself several times.*

turn into VERB

When something **turns into** something else, it becomes that thing.

become
*When water freezes, it **becomes** ice.*

change into
*Caterpillars **change into** butterflies or moths.*

develop into
*Tadpoles soon **develop into** frogs.*

transform into
*With the help of some wings, Rachel was **transformed into** a fairy.*

twist (1) VERB

When you **twist** something, you turn one end in the opposite direction to the other.

coil
*The sailor **coiled** the rope carefully as she got ready to leave.*

curl
*Natalie spent ages **curling** her hair into attractive shapes.*

loop
*The farmer **looped** some wire round the gate to keep it shut.*

turn
*Florence **turned** the handle and pulled the door open.*

wind
*Dad **wound** string round and round the broken chair leg.*

twist (2) VERB

When something **twists**, it moves or bends into a strange shape.

bend
*Sophie's foot slipped on a rock and her ankle **bent** painfully.*

curve
*The road **curved** to the left and suddenly we saw the cottage.*

weave
*Branches of trees **weaved** above our heads, making a shady tunnel.*

wind
*A narrow stream **wound** through the countryside between green meadows.*

zigzag
*Halfway down the mountainside the track **zigzagged**, slowing the car right down.*

typical ADJECTIVE

Something that is **typical** is what you would expect.

average
*An **average** woman needs about 2000 calories a day.*

normal
*For us, a **normal** day starts at 7a.m.*

standard
*His **standard** way of dealing with problems is to ignore them.*

usual
*It was Margaret's **usual** Wednesday visit to the hairdresser.*

Wednesday

Uu

ugly ADJECTIVE

Someone or something that is **ugly** is not pleasant to look at.

hideous
*The ogre gave them a **hideous** grin.*

repulsive
*Christopher opened his present and found a **repulsive** jumper.*

unattractive
*The troll was **unattractive** to say the least.*

→ not much to look at

understand (1) VERB

If you **understand** someone, you know what they mean.

follow
*It was so complicated they couldn't **follow** it at all.*

get
*The others were laughing, but Tom didn't **get** the joke.*

see
*It was difficult, but we soon **saw** what he was getting at.*

take in
*The teacher had to tell her three times before she **took it in**.*

understand (2) VERB

If you **understand** something, you know how or why it is happening.

appreciate
*When they tried ice-skating they **appreciated** how difficult it was.*

fathom
*It's hard to **fathom** how ants communicate, but they do.*

grasp
*Anthony had only just **grasped** how a tin-opener worked.*

realize
*Vicky soon **realized** that nursing is a demanding job.*

understand (3) VERB

To **understand** can mean to hear of something.

believe
*I **believe** you're going up next year?*

gather
*They **gathered** that a new teacher was joining the school.*

hear
*Mum **heard** a new supermarket was opening soon.*

unhappy ADJECTIVE

Someone who is **unhappy** is sad or miserable.

depressed
*He felt **depressed** when he failed the music exam.*

down
*She was feeling **down** about having to move away from her friends.*

miserable
*Dad said he'd had a **miserable** day at work and was glad to be home.*

sad
*They were all **sad** that Great-grandma wasn't well enough to come to the party.*

ANTONYM: happy

a b c d e f g h i j k l m n o p q r s t **Uu** v w x y z

upset (1) ADJECTIVE

If you are **upset**, you are unhappy or disappointed.

distressed
*Miss Muffet was **distressed** when a spider sat down beside her.*

hurt
*Sergei was **hurt** when his sister laughed at him.*

troubled
*My friend seemed **troubled**, so I put an arm round his shoulders.*

unhappy
*Sophie was **unhappy** because her kitten wasn't well.*

upset (2) VERB

If you **upset** someone, you make them worried or unhappy.

bother
*I don't want to **bother** Grandma just now.*

distress
*David was sorry he had **distressed** his Auntie Jo.*

upset (3) VERB

If someone **upsets** something, they turn it over by accident.

knock over
*Nina stumbled against a table and **knocked over** a vase.*

spill
*A toddler **spilt** orange juice right over her homework.*

useful ADJECTIVE

If something is **useful**, it helps you in some way.

handy
*Mum said it would be **handy** to have a robot that did housework.*

helpful
*Robert was given a **helpful** book on camping and some insect repellent.*

practical
*"That rucksack isn't **practical** for hiking," said Dan. "It's too small."*

valuable
*The first-aid box was a **valuable** part of their luggage.*

useless ADJECTIVE

If it is **useless** to do something, it will not achieve anything helpful.

fruitless
*Their search for the missing spade was **fruitless**, and they had to give up.*

futile
*She had a **futile** argument with her dad about staying out late.*

hopeless
*It was **hopeless** trying to work with such poor tools.*

pointless
*"This is a **pointless** discussion," said Mum. "You're not going and that's the end of it."*

ANTONYM: useful

vague

Vv

vague ADJECTIVE

Things that are **vague** are not definite or clear.

dim
*When he woke, Marty had only a **dim** memory of the frightening dream.*

general
*He gave a **general** outline of the project and left us to work out the details.*

hazy
*Mrs Jefferson could give only a **hazy** description of the burglar.*

woolly
*His account of the holiday in Spain was rather **woolly**.*

vain ADJECTIVE

A **vain** person is too proud of how they look or what they can do.

boastful
*Spencer didn't mind sounding **boastful** about his adventures.*

conceited
*I don't want Emma for a friend. She's far too **conceited**.*

proud
*He's too **proud** to admit that he might be wrong.*

valuable (1) ADJECTIVE

Things that are **valuable** are worth a lot of money.

expensive
*Calvin's parents gave him an **expensive** mountain bike.*

precious
*The princess's hand sparkled with **precious** diamonds and emeralds.*

valuable (2) ADJECTIVE

Help or advice that is **valuable** is very useful.

helpful
*Advice from older people can be **helpful**.*

important
*The coach gave her some **important** tips to help improve her swimming.*

useful
*He has lots of **useful** ideas about how to keep plants healthy.*

worthwhile
*The teacher helped him with some **worthwhile** guidance on his project.*

variety (1) NOUN

A **variety** of things is a number of different kinds.

assortment
*There was an **assortment** of biscuits still in the tin.*

collection
*The family had a huge **collection** of books on shelves around the room.*

mixture
*I like to have a **mixture** of chocolates.*

range
*The shop sold a **range** of shampoos.*

variety (2) NOUN

A **variety** is a particular type of something.

class
*There are several different **classes** of butterfly here.*

kind
*She couldn't decide what **kind** of rose to plant by the gate.*

sort
*We've got lots of different apples. Which **sort** do you like best?*

type
*How quickly a plant grows depends on what **type** it is.*

a
b
c
d
e
f
g
h
i
j
k
l
m
n
o
p
q
r
s
t
u
Vv
w
x
y
z

vegetable NOUN

Vegetables are plants, or parts of plants, that can be eaten.

SOME VEGETABLES:

asparagus	onion
aubergine	parsnip
(also known as eggplant)	peas
beans	pepper
cabbage	(also known as capsicum)
carrot	potato
cauliflower	pumpkin
chilli	spinach
courgette	sprouts
(also known as zucchini)	squash
leek	sweet potato
marrow	turnip
mushroom	yam

asparagus

mushrooms

carrots

sweet potato

version NOUN

A **version** of something is a form of it in which some details are different from other forms.

account
Esther's account of the holiday was very different from Charlie's.

description
Everyone gave a different description of the accident.

story
The teacher didn't know whose story she should believe.

victory NOUN

A **victory** is a success in a battle or competition.

success
Supporters cheered the team for its success in the match.

triumph
The slaying of the fearsome dragon was a triumph for the knight.

win
The swimming team had never been beaten and was confident it would have another win.

a
b
c
d
e
f
g
h
i
j
k
l
m
n
o
p
q
r
s
t
u
v
Ww
x
y
z

wait VERB

If you **wait**, you spend time before something happens.

hang on
Hang on! I've got to get my coat.

hold on
*His friends couldn't **hold on** any longer, so they went on ahead.*

stay
*The dog had to **stay** outside the shop.*

walk VERB

When you **walk**, you move along by putting one foot in front of the other.

creep
*They **crept** silently past the sleeping dog.*

dawdle
*The children **dawdled** along the path.*

hike
*Rupert **hiked** for five miles in the hills.*

limp
*One of the elves was **limping** awkwardly.*

march
*Evelyn **marched** along the road in time to the music.*

prowl
*He saw a wolf **prowling** around nearby.*

wander VERB

If you **wander**, you walk around without going in any particular direction.

drift
*We **drifted** from shop to shop without buying anything.*

ramble
*The boys enjoyed **rambling** over the hills, collecting blackberries.*

roam
*Our cat likes to **roam** in the fields and play in the long grass.*

stray
*"Make sure you shut the gates," said the farmer, "or the sheep will **stray**."*

want (1) VERB

If you **want** something, you wish for it.

desire
*The knight **desired** to marry the king's clever daughter.*

fancy
*Mum really **fancied** an iced bun.*

wish for
*Latasha's cousin was given all the things she could possibly **wish for**.*

want (2) VERB

To **want** something can mean to need it for some reason.

be short of
*They discovered they **were short of** dry firewood for the stove.*

need
*Alex's hair **needed** cutting. He could hardly see where he was going.*

require
*An old lady **required** help to get across the busy road.*

warm (1) ADJECTIVE

Something that is **warm** has some heat, but not enough to be hot.

comfortable
His room in the hospital was kept at a comfortable temperature.

cosy
Mark felt cosy under the duvet.

not too hot
Daisy's cocoa was not too hot.

snug
Raju was snug in his winter gear.

warm (2) ADJECTIVE

Someone who is **warm** is friendly and affectionate.

affectionate
Desdemona gave her grandmother an affectionate hug.

cheerful
That lady in the sweetshop is always cheerful and friendly.

friendly
The policeman gave her a friendly smile.

kindly
Our school janitor is a kindly person.

loving
Christopher wrote loving messages in the birthday card.

pleasant
You can be sure of a pleasant welcome in Kate's house.

watch (1) VERB

If you **watch** something, you look at it carefully to see what happens.

gaze at
Hannah gazed at the butterfly as it sipped nectar from the flower.

look at
Robert wanted to look at the cricket match on the green.

observe
The magician told them to observe him very carefully.

see
They tried to see the way the machine worked, but it was too complicated.

stare at
We stared at a spider making its web.

watch (2) VERB

To **watch** can mean to look after something.

guard
The dog could be relied on to guard the house when they were out.

keep an eye on
Charlotte promised to keep an eye on the baby while Mum was upstairs.

look after
Could you please look after the cat while we're out?

mind
Danny offered to mind the shop for half an hour.

take care of
A neighbour took care of the children for the afternoon.

a
b
c
d
e
f
g
h
i
j
k
l
m
n
o
p
q
r
s
t
u
v
Ww
x
y
z

water

NOUN

Water is a clear liquid that all living things need in order to live.

LARGE AREAS OF WATER:
lake   reservoir
ocean   sea

SMALL AREAS OF WATER:
pond   puddle
pool

WATER FLOWING BETWEEN BANKS:
brook   river
canal   stream

FALLING WATER:
cascade   waterfall
cataract   weir

RACING WATER:
rapids

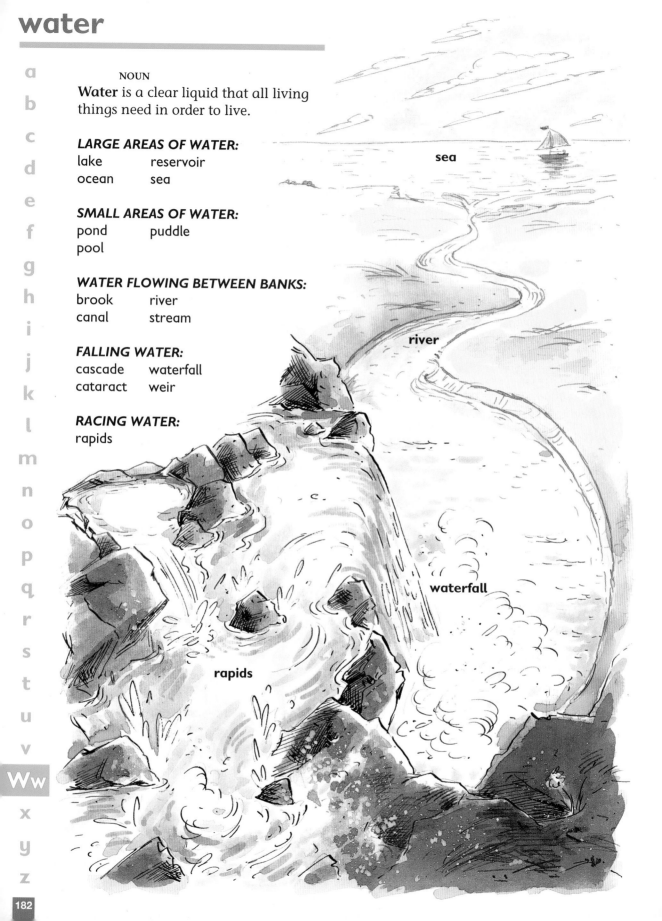

sea

river

waterfall

rapids

way (1) NOUN

The **way** to a particular place is the direction you have to go to get there.

direction
We turned left, but soon found it was the wrong direction.

lane
"I'm sure this is the right lane," Graham said at last.

path
They came to a fork and weren't sure which path to choose.

road
"Is this the road to the Town Hall?" asked Dick importantly.

route
Dad was so keen to try out his brand-new car that he drove the long route to Granny's house.

track
The track to the farm was easy to find, but it was very muddy.

way (2) NOUN

A **way** of doing something is how it can be done.

fashion
"We'll never do it if we carry on in this fashion," said Dad.

manner
Albert approached every problem in a calm manner.

means
They tried every means they could think of to get him out of bed.

method
There were several methods of doing it. Sophie chose the simplest.

system
"This system will work," said Tom. "Just give it a chance."

technique
The plumber showed us a technique to stop the leak.

weak (1) ADJECTIVE

People or animals that are **weak** do not have much strength or energy.

delicate
Louise was delicate as a young child.

feeble
Mum said she was feeling much too feeble to go swimming.

frail
The old man was too frail to carry his shopping home.

puny
Sita chose the puniest puppy of the litter.

sickly
"Actually I feel rotten," said Ben, and gave a sickly smile.

ANTONYM: **strong**

weak (2) ADJECTIVE

If an object or part of an object is **weak**, it could break easily.

flimsy
The boat looked too flimsy to take the whole family.

fragile
Ranjit's new toy was so fragile it broke in the first ten minutes.

rickety
The chair looked nice, but one of the legs was rickety.

ANTONYM: **strong**

weak (3) ADJECTIVE

Drinks that are **weak** do not have a strong taste.

diluted
Lizzie complained that her orange squash was too diluted.

tasteless
The tea in the cafe was tasteless.

thin
The tomato soup was so thin it was more like water.

a
b
c
d
e
f
g
h
i
j
k
l
m
n
o
p
q
r
s
t
u
v
Ww
x
y
z

weather

weather NOUN

The **weather** is what it is like outside, for example raining, sunny or windy.

WEATHER WORDS: ADJECTIVES

changeable weather
breezy   showery

cold weather
bitter   freezing   icy
cold   frosty   snowy

dull weather
chilly   cool   foggy
cloudy   drizzly   misty

stormy weather
thundery   windy

sunny weather
bright   fine   sunny
clear   hot   warm
dry

→ boiling hot; scorching hot

wet weather
damp   rainy

WEATHER WORDS: NOUNS

changeable weather
breeze   showers
rainbow   sunshine

hot weather
drought   heatwave   sun

stormy weather
blizzard   hail   storm
gale   lightning   thunder
gust   snowstorm   wind

wet weather
downpour   sleet
rain   wet

WEATHER WORDS: VERBS

wet weather
drizzle   pour   rain

→ bucket down; rain cats and dogs

weird ADJECTIVE
Something that is **weird** seems strange and peculiar.

curious
*They were on the way to school when a **curious** thing happened.*

extraordinary
*Suddenly an **extraordinary** bird appeared in the garden.*

funny
*"That's **funny**," said Mum. "I made twelve cakes. Now there are only ten."*

odd
*They heard an **odd** creaking sound coming from the cellar, and looked at each other in alarm.*

peculiar
*The stone was covered in **peculiar** marks, like ancient writing.*

strange
*Today a **strange** notice appeared in the sweetshop window.*

unusual
*The woman was wearing an **unusual** hat.*

→ spooky

wet (1) ADJECTIVE
If something is **wet**, it is covered in water or other liquid.

damp
*The ground was **damp**, so they sat on a waterproof rug.*

drenched
*Holly was **drenched** by the time she got to school.*

moist
*Robin checked that the soil in the plant pot was **moist**.*

soaked
*Lizzie wished she'd worn boots. Her trainers were **soaked**.*

→ like a drowned rat; soaked to the skin

ANTONYM: dry

wet (2) ADJECTIVE
If the weather is **wet**, it is raining.

drizzly
*It was **drizzly** outside, but not worth taking an umbrella.*

misty
*The **misty** air left droplets of water on leaves and flowers.*

rainy
*It was a **rainy** Sunday afternoon, and Sanjay was bored.*

showery
*Julia's jacket was great for **showery** weather, although it was starting to get a bit small.*

stormy
*We only had one day of **stormy** weather before the canal flooded.*

ANTONYM: dry or fine

wet (3) VERB
If you **wet** something, you put liquid on it.

dampen
*Gran always **dampens** her washing before she irons it.*

drown
*The river burst its banks and **drowned** Anastasia's garden for the second time in a year.*

soak
*The ride at the theme park **soaked** Mum through to the skin.*

spatter
*The dog shook itself vigorously and **spattered** everybody.*

splash
*A passing car **splashed** Emily from head to foot.*

water
*Make sure you **water** the soil around the new plants.*

ANTONYM: dry

wicked

wicked ADJECTIVE
Someone or something **wicked** is very bad.

evil
*There is an **evil** witch in the story of Hansel and Gretel.*

foul
*"Who has done this **foul** deed?" cried the angry king.*

vicious
*He was a cruel and **vicious** man.*

vile
*Many **vile** things happen during a war.*

wild (1) ADJECTIVE
Wild animals, birds and plants live in natural surroundings and are not looked after by people.

free
*Many colourful birds fly **free** in rainforests.*

natural
*In the countryside, plants and insects live in **natural** conditions.*

untamed
*In some places, horses run **untamed**.*

wild (2) ADJECTIVE
If the weather is **wild**, it is rough and stormy.

rough
*The boat was tossed around on **rough** seas.*

stormy
*It was a **stormy** night and the lifeboat crew was ready for trouble.*

violent
*A **violent** storm swept the island.*

wild (3) ADJECTIVE
Wild behaviour is not controlled.

boisterous
*All the children became **boisterous** when their team won.*

chaotic
***Chaotic** scenes greeted Mrs Jones when she came back into the room.*

noisy
*The class was so **noisy** the teacher couldn't make herself heard.*

rough
*Some of the games got a bit **rough**.*

rowdy
*My dad's strict and he won't put up with **rowdy** behaviour.*

willing ADJECTIVE
If you are **willing** to do something, you are ready and happy to do it.

eager
*William was **eager** to help wash the car.*

happy
*Emma said she'd be **happy** to get her grandmother's shopping.*

prepared
*Josh said he was **prepared** to do the washing-up for a week.*

ready
*Rob was always **ready** to take the dog for a walk.*

ANTONYM: **unwilling**

win (1) VERB

If you **win** a race or game, you do better than the others taking part.

come first
"Did you come first?" asked the coach.

succeed
Lisa entered the painting competition, determined to succeed.

triumph
Tweedledum was determined to triumph in the battle against his brother.

ANTONYM: **lose**

win (2) VERB

If you **win** something such as a prize, you get it for doing something well.

earn
Rachel was delighted to earn herself a place in the team.

get
Jeremy got a prize for swimming.

receive
Indigo received a cup for being Student of the Year.

secure
My brother finally secured a place in the football team.

wind VERB

If a road or river **winds**, it has lots of bends in it.

curve
Further along, the river curves round a steep bank.

snake
The road snakes to and fro along the edge of the cliff.

turn
In the middle of the wood the path suddenly turns off to the left.

twist
The lane twists dangerously here, so drivers have to be extra careful.

wipe VERB

If you **wipe** something, you rub its surface lightly to remove dirt or liquid.

dry
I quickly dried the table with a tissue to get rid of the spilt milk.

dust
There was no time to dust the sideboard before the visitors arrived.

mop
We had to mop the kitchen floor after we'd tramped through in our football boots.

polish
Dad polished his favourite shoes ready for the interview.

rub
"You'll have to rub a bit harder than that," said Mum.

wise ADJECTIVE

If someone tells you it would be **wise** to do something, they mean it would be sensible.

intelligent
I think the intelligent thing to do would be to go straight home.

reasonable
We thought it was reasonable at the time.

sensible
She couldn't decide what would be a sensible course of action.

ANTONYM: **foolish**

wither VERB

If a plant **withers**, it shrivels up and dies.

droop
*Dad rushed out to water the flowers because they were **drooping**.*

dry up
*All my seedlings **dried up** in the sun.*

shrink
*In the drought, the runner beans **shrank** to half their normal size.*

shrivel
*The leaves on the tree **shrivelled** instead of turning a glorious red.*

wilt
*She put the wrong food on the houseplant and it soon began to **wilt**.*

wobble VERB

If something **wobbles**, it makes small movements from side to side.

shake
*The table **shook** every time Dad tried to write his list of things to fix.*

tremble
*His knees **trembled** with fear.*

vibrate
*Whenever a lorry went past, everything on the shelf **vibrated**.*

work (1) VERB

When you **work**, you spend time and energy doing something useful.

labour
*Cinderella was expected to **labour** all day for the ugly sisters.*

slave
*The witch said she was tired of **slaving** over a hot cauldron.*

slog INFORMAL
*Emily always seemed to be **slogging** away at something or other.*

toil
*All day, Grandpa **toiled** in the hot sun.*

work (2) VERB

If something **works**, it does what it is supposed to do.

function
*Gus complained his computer wasn't **functioning** properly.*

go
*Esther shook her watch, trying to make it **go**.*

run
*The car **ran** well after the mechanic had mended it.*

work (3) NOUN

Work can be someone's job.

business
*His **business** is mainly buying and selling computers.*

career
*My sister's **career** as a pilot takes her all over the world.*

craft
*The **craft** that Uncle Freddy enjoys best is woodcarving.*

job
*Alison is hoping that her new **job** will be better paid.*

profession
*Doctor Collins says he feels his **profession** is worthwhile.*

trade
*Our plumber is proud of his **trade**.*

worry (1) VERB

If you **worry**, you keep thinking about problems or about unpleasant things that might happen.

be anxious
You can tell that my brother is anxious about his piano exam.

brood
Surely you're not still brooding about what she said?

feel uneasy
She was feeling uneasy about making the journey on her own.

fret
Please stop fretting! You can't change anything now.

worry (2) VERB

If you **worry** someone, you disturb them with a problem.

bother
Don't bother me now. I'm just going out.

hassle INFORMAL
Your sister says you keep hassling her.

pester
I wish they'd stop pestering me.

plague
My brother said I should work it out for myself and not plague him with questions.

trouble
"I hate to trouble you," said Mum, "but shouldn't you be doing some homework?"

wrong (1) ADJECTIVE

Something that is **wrong** is not correct.

false
She couldn't decide if he gave a false answer on purpose.

faulty
The wiring on that iron is faulty. It could be dangerous.

incorrect
In general the story is true, but some of the details are incorrect.

mistaken
I'm sure you're mistaken. That couldn't have been Spencer.

untrue
Jasper's story about his dad being an astronaut was quite untrue.

→ wide of the mark

ANTONYM:

wrong (2) ADJECTIVE

If a person does something **wrong**, they do something bad.

bad
The way the ugly sisters treated Cinderella was bad.

crooked
Using stolen credit cards is a crooked way to behave.

dishonest
Beth knew it was dishonest to ride on a train without paying.

wicked
It was wicked to give Snow White a poisoned apple.

a
b
c
d
e
f
g
h
i
j
k
l
m
n
o
p
q
r
s
t
u
v
Ww
x
y
z

Xx Yy Zz

young (1) ADJECTIVE

A **young** person, animal or plant has not been alive for very long.

adolescent
*Two **adolescent** boys ran to help the old lady when she fell.*

fresh
*Mum went to the vegetable garden to cut a **fresh** lettuce.*

immature
*My older sister can behave in a very **immature** way.*

infant
*Joshua just didn't want to play with his **infant** friends.*

junior
*The youth club has plenty of things for **junior** members to do.*

little
*Outside the shop a **little** boy was crying. He said he was lost.*

teenage
*Holly scanned the library shelves for **teenage** fiction.*

unfledged
*Mary found an **unfledged** bird on the ground. It had fallen from its nest.*

youthful
*My dad must be quite old, although he still looks **youthful**.*

ANTONYM: old

young (2) PLURAL NOUN

The **young** of an animal are its babies.

brood
*The mother hen gathered her **brood** under her wings.*

family
*Our cat has four new kittens and is very proud of her **family**.*

litter
*Star's **litter** occupied the whole basket and some of the kitchen floor.*

offspring
*Female animals are usually very protective of their **offspring**.*

YOUNG ANIMALS:

A young bear is a cub.
A young cat is a kitten.
A young chicken is a chick.
A young cow is a calf.
A young deer is a fawn.
A young dog is a puppy.
A young duck is a duckling.
A young elephant is a calf.
A young fox is a cub.
A young goat is a kid.
A young goose is a gosling.
A young hare is a leveret.
A young horse is a foal.
A young kangaroo is a joey.
A young lion is a cub.
A young pig is a piglet.
A young rabbit is a kitten.
A young seal is a calf or pup.
A young sheep is a lamb.
A young swan is a cygnet.
A young tiger is a cub.
A young whale is a calf.
A young wolf is a cub.

SOME MOTHERS AND YOUNG:

bear and cub

cat and kitten

deer and fawn

horse and foal

kangaroo and joey

goat and kid

pig and piglet

rabbit and kitten

tiger and cub

whale and calf

zero NOUN

You can use **zero** to mean none at all.

nil

*They knew their chances of Dad taking them to the cinema were **nil** unless they promised to behave.*

none at all

*Old Mother Hubbard looked for food in her cupboard, but there was **none at all**.*

nothing

*There was **nothing** Jackie could find to wear for the evening out.*

zigzag VERB

If something **zigzags**, it goes in a line that keeps changing direction sharply.

bend

*Rory tried to draw a straight line, but it **bent** all over the place.*

twist

*The road **twisted** dangerously and Dad found it hard to control the car.*

wind

*A narrow track **wound** across the field. It was made by sheep and goats.*

A–Z Index

See 'Using the index' for instructions on how to use this synonym index.

Bb

chew . . . . **eat** 44
chief . . . . **basic** 13
chief . . . . **main** 100
chilly . . . . **cold** 29
chink . . . . **gap** 62
chink . . . . **leak** 96
chink . . . . **opening** 113
chip . . . . **bit** 17
chip . . . . **break** 20
chip . . . . **damage** 36
chirpy . . . . **lively** 97
choke . . . . **gasp** 62
choose . . . . **pick** 116
chop . . . . **cut** 35
chore . . . . **job** 89
chunk . . . . **bit** 17
chunk . . . . **lump** 99
civil . . . . **polite** 120
claim . . . . **say** 132
clamber . . . . **climb** 28
clash . . . . **crash** 33
clasp . . . . **hold** 80
clasp . . . . **take** 160
class . . . . **variety** 178
clatter . . . . **crash** 33
clatter . . . . **noise** 111
claw . . . . **tear** 162
clean . . . . **fresh** 58
clean . . . . **pure** 123
clear . . . . **easy** 44
clear . . . . **empty** 45
clear . . . . **fresh** 58
clear . . . . **plain** 118
clear . . . . **pure** 123
clear out . . . . **empty** 45

clear up . . . . **solve** 146
clever . . . . **bright** 21
clever . . . . **good** 67
clever . . . . **sharp** 139
clever . . . . **smart** 144
climb . . . . **rise** 128
climbing the
  walls . . . . **angry** 9
clip . . . . **cut** 35
cloak . . . . **cover** 33
cloak and
  dagger . . . . **secret** 134
close . . . . **finish** 54
close . . . . **friendly** 59
close . . . . **shut** 141
close . . . . **stuffy** 157
closing . . . . **last** 94
clothing . . . . **clothes** 28
cloudless . . . . **clear** 27
cloudy . . . . **dull** 43
clout . . . . **hit** 79
clutch . . . . **grab** 68
clutch . . . . **hold** 80
clutch . . . . **seize** 135
clutter . . . . **mess** 104
coat . . . . **layer** 95
coating . . . . **layer** 95
coax . . . . **persuade** 115
code . . . . **law** 95
coil . . . . **twist** 175
coincidence . . . . . **accident** 8
cold-hearted . . . . **cruel** 34
collage . . . . **picture** 116
collapse . . . . **fall** 50
collect . . . . **gather** 63

collect

difficult

elegant

Ee

excellent	**great**	69
exceptional	**strange**	154
exchange	**change**	26
exciting	**good**	67
exciting	**interesting**	87
exclaim	**say**	132
excursion	**journey**	90
excursion	**trip**	172
execute	**kill**	92
exert yourself	**struggle**	156
exhausted	**tired**	169
exhausting	**hard**	76
exhibit	**show**	141
exhibition	**show**	141
expand	**grow**	72
expand	**increase**	85
expedition	**journey**	90
expensive	**valuable**	178
experience	**feel**	52
experience	**have**	77
expert	**good**	67
explain	**demonstrate**	37
explain	**show**	140
explain	**solve**	146
explode	**burst**	23
explosion	**bang**	13
express	**fast**	51
extend	**increase**	85
exterminate	**kill**	92
extraordinary	**different**	38
extraordinary	**special**	149
extraordinary	**strange**	155
extraordinary	**weird**	185

Ff

fabulous	**good**	67
facts	**information**	86
facts	**knowledge**	93
factual	**true**	173
faded	**faint**	48
faded	**pale**	114
faint	**misty**	106
faint	**soft**	145
fair	**light**	97
fairly	**quite**	125
fake	**copy**	32
fake	**false**	50
fall	**trip**	172
fall about laughing	**laugh**	95
fall apart	**break**	20
false	**wrong**	189
family	**young**	190
famished	**hungry**	82
famous	**great**	69
famous	**important**	85
fanciful	**imaginary**	84
fancy	**want**	180
fantastic	**great**	69
fantasy	**dream**	42
fascinating	**interesting**	87
fascinating	**magical**	100
fashion	**way**	183
fast	**quick**	124
fasten	**fix**	55
fasten	**hang**	75
fasten	**shut**	141
fasten	**tie**	167

flimsy . . . . **light** 97
flimsy . . . . **thin** 165
flimsy . . . . **weak** 183
fling . . . . **move** 107
fling . . . . **scatter** 133
fling . . . . **throw** 166
flock . . . . **gather** 63
flood . . . . **flow** 55
flourish . . . . **grow** 72
flourish . . . . **shake** 137
flowing . . . . **graceful** 68
fluffy . . . . **soft** 145
fluid . . . . **juice** 91
flutter . . . . **fly** 57
fly . . . . **hurry** 82
fly . . . . **move** 107
foam . . . . . . **boil** 19
fold . . . . . . **bend** 15
follow . . . . . . **chase** 26
follow . . . . . . **copy** 32
follow . . . . . . **see** 135
follow . . . . . . **understand** 176
fool . . . . **trick** 172
foolish . . . . . . **silly** 142
foolish . . . . . . **stupid** 157
foot . . . . **bottom** 19
forbid . . . . . . **ban** 13
force . . . . **drive** 43
force . . . . . . **effort** 45
force . . . . . . **make** 100
force . . . . . . **power** 121
force . . . . . . **push** 123
force . . . . . . **thrust** 167
foreign . . . . . . **strange** 155
forged . . . . . . **false** 50

forgery . . . . **copy** 32
forlorn . . . . **lonely** 98
form . . . . **make** 100
form . . . . **shape** 138
foul . . . . **dirty** 39
foul . . . . **wicked** 186
foundation . . . . . . **bottom** 19
fountain . . . . . . **jet** 88
fragile . . . . . . **weak** 183
fragment . . . . . . **bit** 17
fragment . . . . . . **part** 114
fragrance . . . . . . **smell** 144
frail . . . . . . **fragile** 58
frail . . . . . . **weak** 183
free . . . . . . **save** 131
free . . . . . . **wild** 186
freezing . . . . . . **cold** 29
frequently . . . . . . **often** 112
fresh . . . . . . **young** 190
fret . . . . . . **worry** 189
friendless . . . . . . **lonely** 98
friendly . . . . . . **helpful** 78
friendly . . . . . . **informal** 86
friendly . . . . . . **kind** 93
friendly . . . . . . **nice** 110
friendly . . . . . . **pleasant** 119
friendly . . . . . . **warm** 181
fright . . . . . . **fear** 52
frighten . . . . . . **bully** 23
frighten . . . . . . **disturb** 40
frighten . . . . . . **scare** 133
frightening . . . . . . **dreadful** 42
frightful . . . . . . **dreadful** 42
frisky . . . . . . **lively** 97
frosty . . . . . . **cold** 29

Hh

Ii

Mm

Pp

Qq

Ss

Tt